VGM Opportunities Series

OPPORTUNITIES IN
TECHNICAL
EDUCATION
CAREERS

Robert Connelly

Foreword by
Roger Speer
Director
Universal Technical Institute

VGM Career Horizons
NTC/Contemporary Publishing Company

Library of Congress Cataloging-in-Publication Data

Connelly, Robert, 1950–
    Opportunities in technical education / Robert Connelly : foreword
by Roger Speer.
        p.   cm. — (VGM opportunities series)
    ISBN 0-8442-2310-7 (cloth). — ISBN 0-8442-2311-5 (pbk.)
    1. Technical education—Vocational guidance—United States.
I. Title. II. Series.
T73.C5953   1997
607.1'5—dc21   97-29001
                                                                CIP

Published by VGM Career Horizons
An imprint of NTC/Contemporary Publishing Company
4255 West Touhy Avenue, Lincolnwood (Chicago), Illinois 60646-1975 U.S.A.
Copyright © 1998 by NTC/Contemporary Publishing Company
Manufactured in the United States of America
International Standard Book Number: 0-8442-2310-7; 0-8442-2311-5 (soft)
15   14   13   12   11   10   9   8   7   6   5   4   3   2   1

CONTENTS

ABOUT THE AUTHOR

Bob Connelly is the director of the Young Adult Program, an alternative education program in the northwest suburbs of Chicago, Illinois. He earned both his bachelor's and master's degrees in education from Northern Illinois University, where he studied Foundations of Education under the direction of Dr. Nolan Armstrong. Mr. Connelly has presented numerous papers on serving at-risk youth at state and national conferences, and he is the former editor of *Alternative Education: The Journal of the Illinois Alternative Education Association.*

FOREWORD

There's a quote from Roger Mager that I love to use when people ask me about vocational education. It goes like this:

> Vocational and technical education is an act of humanity. It is the attempt to enrich the lives of others by expanding their ability to deal more successfully with the world in which they live. The measure of our success is the degree to which we can make our graduates more employable, self-sufficient, and socially adept. There are few callings more personally rewarding than contributing to the success of others.

I really believe that. At our school, we see ourselves as the link between high school and industry. We provide opportunities and challenges for young people, so they can develop the technical and professional skills they need to build a future in a field that is rich with opportunities.

If you are interested in working with young people and enjoy the excitement of technology, use this book to learn more about today's most challenging and rewarding careers.

Roger Speer
Director
Universal Technical Institute
Glendale Heights, Illinois

PREFACE

There is no question that technology is transforming our world, but no matter how pervasive the changes are, one thing will remain constant: We will always need capable, caring people to teach us how to use the new tools technology brings us. People who are interested in technology and who enjoy working with student and adult learners can use this book to get information about teaching careers in technology. There will be growing opportunities for teaching careers in high school, college, proprietary schools, media and information, and business and industry. The first half of this book features chapters on each of these specific careers. For a real-life look at the field, each chapter opens with interviews with working professionals. The second half of the book includes advice on student teaching, preparing resumes, and conducting interviews. There are also comprehensive resources that will help readers to select colleges for training, prepare resumes, and begin a job search.

Helping people learn new skills is one of the most challenging careers that exists. At the same time, it is one of the most rewarding fields that anyone can enter. I hope this book will help people who are committed to this challenge.

CHAPTER 1

TEACHING TECHNOLOGY IN HIGH SCHOOL

BUSINESS, TECHNOLOGY, AND LIFE STUDIES DEPARTMENT CHAIR

Mark Koch is the department chair for the Business, Technology, and Life Studies Department at Rolling Meadows High School in Rolling Meadows, Illinois.

What kind of academic and work experiences did the most to prepare you for your role as a department chair?

My work experience in industry was very important to me. It not only added some distance in age between myself and my students, but it was useful to have real-life experiences in the work world to draw on.

How did you become interested in school administration?

I wanted to have more of my ideas taken seriously, and I wanted the support from the administration to make that happen.

What kind of preparation would you recommend for someone who is interested in school administration?

I would strongly recommend that people who are interested in this field work on organizational skills. In this job, you seem to need to

be able to do six things at the same time. Unless you are very organized, your workday will disappear before you have time to do any
of the things you think are really important. Communication and
human relations skills are also critical. Your main task is to develop
a vision of where you want your division to go. To make that vision
happen, you need to communicate the vision and involve staff
members who are critical to the program's success. You have to
learn to be patient with students and staff and to not take yourself
too seriously. You have to be willing to listen to people and be
objective. Your colleagues may have a different vision of the way
they want the department to work, and their vision might be the
best choice.

**How would you describe a typical workday? What kinds of
activities tend to dominate your day?**

There is no typical workday. I usually juggle the two classes that I
teach along with short-, medium-, and long-range plans. Everything is usually interrupted by things that arise on a day-to-day
basis.

**What are the kinds of qualifications that you look for when
screening resumes for potential interviews?**

I look for applicants who have amassed a variety of work, education, and life experiences. I want to work with people who can
demonstrate that they are willing to keep up with the new events in
technology. I look for someone who is willing to learn new teaching techniques and who has developed the "people skills" to get
along with students and peers. I don't want to work with a prima
donna.

**If you could give a potential teacher some advice on becoming
an excellent teacher, what would you suggest?**

A strong teacher in this field is going to have computer/technical
work experience. I would suggest that a beginning teacher learn
how to work with unmotivated students. Good teachers also have a

sense of humor and are willing to appreciate and laugh with their colleagues and students on a daily basis.

A high school department chair has many important responsibilities. In most high schools, department chairs teach at least one class; hire, supervise, and evaluate their staff; and provide leadership on important school and school district projects, such as curriculum development or school reform. Department chairs handle student discipline referrals from their teachers, mediate conflicts between parents and teachers, and monitor complaints on working conditions, sexual harassment, and work rules.

The role of teacher/administrator can be a difficult one to fulfill. As a teacher, the department chair must plan instructional activities, motivate students to perform well, and assess their progress. As an administrator, a department chair must enforce school policy, maintain standards for professional conduct, help teachers set goals for themselves, and measure their progress. Supervising second-year or probationary teachers brings the added stress of deciding whether to grant a teacher tenure or to dismiss the teacher. Dealing with adults in a department can be every bit as challenging as dealing with students in a classroom.

As school administrators, department chairs are expected to put in long hours of work, and they are not paid for overtime. In general, department chairs are always paid more than the teachers that they supervise, and they have many school holidays and enjoy an extended break during the summer. People who are drawn to school administration often have a strong desire to make schools work more effectively, especially for students who are not successful in traditional school settings. In order to qualify for this position, applicants must have a bachelor's degree in education and a teaching certificate, or an academic degree from an accredited college or university and a teaching certificate. Applicants must also hold an administrative certificate, and they often have earned a master's degree in school administration or a master's degree in curriculum and supervision. It is very unusual for administrators to be hired directly out of college. In general, all administrators have experience as teachers or counselors before they become administrators. School administration is complex, and schools are hesitant to hire applicants who do not have firsthand classroom experience. Successful administrators have developed strong communication and organizational skills. A sense of humor and a genuine concern for young people are important qualities to bring to this job.

Most schools have very few administrators because they rely on the professionalism of their staff to make the schools run smoothly. There are roughly 349,000 school administrators in the United States. The demand for school administrators will grow slowly as administrators retire and as the school-age population continues to expand. Salaries for school administrators varies from school district to school district, but the national average salary for school administrators is $49,000.

HIGH SCHOOL TECHNOLOGY TEACHER

Art Weidner is a technology teacher for the Business, Technology, and Life Studies Department at Rolling Meadows High School in Rolling Meadows, Illinois.

What advice would you give to people who think that they might be interested in a career in technology education?

I would tell them to be prepared for a major commitment of time and energy. Some people think that they might like to teach because they have this idea that high school teachers work from eight to four and have all summer off. If you want to teach in this field, you have to be available whenever the students are. That might mean evenings, weekends, school holidays, or before school meets.

Why do we have to be so available? The basic reason is that many parents want their kids to take a college preparatory curriculum, and that curriculum doesn't leave much time in a student's schedule for any elective courses. Kids have to choose between band and art and vocal music and technology. If you're teaching technology and you want to work with these kids, you have to be available when they are, and that means a nontraditional schedule. After school or evening classes or classes that meet before the school day starts allow kids to expand their schedules to include technology.

Right now our students are working on the U.S. First robotics competition. We are working with partners from Motorola who volunteer their time during the evening to coach our students. It's very exciting to see our students test their limits in a competition like this. Time after time I hear kids saying, "I didn't know that I was this smart," or "I'll bet you never thought that I was this smart." This is a wonderful opportunity for these kids, but in order to make it work, you have to be in school to supervise, encourage, and help. That means you're in school from seven in the morning until nine at night. And you have to be there because you want to be there, not because somebody's watching over your shoulder.

What kind of preparation would you recommend for someone who is interested in this field of teaching?

In order to work with high school students, you will need to earn a teaching certificate. While you are in college, taking the classes you need for your certificate, try to get certified in as many different teaching areas as you can. Investing the time and money to become certified in several different areas makes you much more employable. Remember that most high schools have salary schedules that are based on education and experience. If you have an undergraduate degree and then go back for a master's degree in another area, you are more expensive to hire than a teacher who has an undergraduate degree but can teach in several different areas.

Experience is also very important. Most people who go into teaching were good students and liked school. It's hard for them to work with students who don't like school and who aren't good students. Tutoring, coaching, and part-time teaching can help new teachers deal with the kinds of motivation and discipline problems that they'll face on the job. Experience in industry is also very helpful, especially when it's time to develop or rework the curriculum.

What qualities would you look for in a good teacher?

Good teachers enjoy working with kids and are willing to keep learning. A good work ethic is very important, too. Good teachers are also very organized. This field changes all the time, and you have to keep up with the changes or your program will die. You need to be willing to work hard and invest long hours in your students. You need to be able to explain the same thing eighteen different ways until it makes sense to the student you're working with. You need to be so well organized that you can get a class started, listen to an excuse for late work, take attendance, and solve a discipline problem all at the same time. You need to be so focused that you can teach a beginning section and an advanced section of a class at the same time and in the same room.

Good teachers need to be self-motivated. Nobody's looking over your shoulder to check on your work, which is nice, but at the same time, nobody's around to tell you what a great job you're doing. Motivation has to come from your own sense of accomplishment. Probably the most important quality is the ability to work with kids who don't like school and don't want to be there. It's hard to focus on a kid's potential when the kid is a discipline problem day after day. Good teachers don't give up easily. Anybody can teach a class of nice, polite kids who want to make their teacher happy. Good teachers are the ones who don't give up on troubled kids.

How would you describe a typical day at school?

I meet five classes a day. I teach in a couple different areas, so the material is different from class to class. I present material, I supervise projects, I work with counselors and parents, and I coach kids on the U.S. First competition. On some days I spend time on committee work to change the way our school day is organized. I work on a committee that wants to change the way we teach technology, so students are better prepared for work when they graduate.

What would you describe as the biggest frustrations in your job?

Anybody who teaches will talk about the frustration they have with parents who can't give their kids the kind of support they need. We have kids who come to school exhausted because they work after school until late at night. We have kids who have never learned any kind of self-discipline at home, and who just get lost here. We have kids whose parents pull them out of school to baby-sit for younger siblings even when it really hurts their work at school. A lot of it is economics. Parents are really pushed and they don't have the time to supervise their kids, to make sure the homework is done or that kids make education a priority. My other frustration is that we don't allow kids enough time in their schedules to take some classes that they might enjoy. The college prep curriculum ties kids up, and in many cases, parents want their kids in these classes when they aren't planning to go on to college. I think we could do a much better job of preparing kids for work if we had the opportunity to work with them. Probably the biggest frustration anybody in teaching faces is in working with kids who just seem to be drifting by and who need to be connected to the school. You have this sense that these kids could get so much out of the four years that they spend here, if somebody could just turn them around. Sometimes we're successful, and those success stories are really neat; but there are kids that we just can't reach, and those are the kids you worry about.

When I started in this business, you had kids who wanted to work with their hands and be able to move around in class. They took auto shop or wood shop or printing or machine shop. It gave them something to look forward to every day. But now, everybody wants to go to college, and nobody's got time for shop classes. If you want to offer electronics, you've got to combine it with something else so that there are enough kids to fill a class. It's like trying to teach band and English in the same classroom at the same time.

There is no question that technology has changed the traditional shop class at high school. Practical arts programs that were dying are reinvigorated by the interest in computers, telecommunications, robotics, and technology. But two points that Mr. Weidner raised are still true: high school technology teachers still work with students who like to move around and work with their hands, and they still need to be very flexible and willing to teach in more than one specialty area.

Teaching at the high school level is very challenging work, but for people who are interested in technology and who enjoy working with young people, high school teaching can be a very rewarding career. In order to prepare for this career, it is necessary to earn a bachelor's degree from an accredited college or university with a major in technology, computers, industrial technology, or electronics. State and provincial laws require that all potential teachers be licensed, and this requires course work and student teaching experiences that lead to earning a teaching certificate. Many states and provinces also require competency testing to guarantee that teachers have a minimum level of skills in math, English, and the humanities.

While academic credentials are important, prospective teachers also need to develop strong communication skills. Teachers need to explain complex information, resolve conflicts, and deal effectively with students, parents, and administrators. Effective teachers need organizational skills that will allow them to keep their students on task, even when students are working on different projects or at a different pace. Supervising a group of students requires great concentration. Teachers are responsible for student safety and attendance as well as student achievement. Teachers frequently compare their job to juggling several projects at once.

Two of the most important tasks that any teacher will face are determining what skills and knowledge students will need to learn and developing the projects, assignments, and activities that will allow them to meet these goals. This process of curriculum development is an ongoing part of a teacher's work. Teachers must also meet the challenge of motivating disaffected students who, because of family issues, economic problems, or personal crises, are unable to focus on school work. Working with young people requires a sense of mission and compassion. The most successful teachers are people who enjoy working with young people more than they care about the subject matter; people who teach kids, not school.

High school teachers often have the opportunity to participate in co-curricular programs at their school, serving as coaches, activity sponsors, and music and theater directors. These opportunities typically include stipends to compensate the teacher for the additional time spent at school. High school teachers enjoy an academic schedule that allows for extended vacation time to use for additional professional growth or for time with friends and family. Salaries for high school teachers vary widely from school district to school district, but they average $34,000 per year. Salaries tend to increase based on continued education and experience and range upwards to $80,000 in some affluent school districts.

Opportunities for high school technology teachers will increase due to the rising number of school-age children and because of the expanding interest in technology. Teacher retirements will also create opportunities.

KEYBOARDING TEACHER

Marilyn Donovan teaches keyboarding and cooperative education at Rolling Meadows High School in Rolling Meadows, Illinois.

How did you become interested in technology?

I became interested as new developments occurred in word processing, starting with electric typewriters, stand-alone work processing, and finally computers.

Why did you decide to become a teacher?

I worked as a secretary for seven years and decided that I wanted to teach other office skills. I learned office skills from experience, and

I thought that I would like to help young people learn these skills before they entered the job market.

How would you describe a typical workday? What kinds of activities tend to dominate your day?

I teach keyboarding for three class periods every day. I grade papers for one and a half to two hours every day. The remaining part of my workday is spent coordinating satellite programs for work study and teacher aide preparation.

If someone asked for your advice on how to become a good teacher, what skills and qualities would you suggest that they try to develop?

Teachers have a powerful influence on their students. They need to make a genuine effort to be fair to these students. Kids can tell if you have favorites, and they resent it very much. We all need to work on staying open-minded. There are lots of ways to approach problems, and we have to be careful not to fall into a "they've always done it this way" syndrome. We also must remember to treat students with kindness and respect. Even the most challenging students respond to a caring, interested teacher. We need to emphasize the positive things that students do, and whenever possible, we need to relate the activities that we do in class to real-life activities.

What is the most challenging part of your job?

I would call it a tie between keeping up with the paperwork and dealing with extreme behavior problems. The extreme behavior problems take such a disproportionate amount of my time and energy that I worry about shortchanging my other students.

What class or experience was most helpful to you in becoming a good teacher?

I think that my special education and psychology classes were a big help for me, but overall experience is also helpful. I have learned a lot from my students over the last twenty-four years—especially from my mistakes.

If you could change one part of your job description, what would you add or delete?

I would eliminate a lot of the paperwork. Progress reports and notices to parents take a huge amount of time.

When you started teaching, was there one suggestion or piece of advice that you wish someone had given you?

When I first started teaching, I was very idealistic. There were several older teachers who couldn't wait to shoot down every idea I had on units that I wanted to teach. I wish that someone would have encouraged me to try the new things I wanted to do instead of discouraging me. I had a lot of enthusiasm that the other teachers seemed to resent.

Many school districts acknowledge the importance of computer education by requiring keyboarding for all high school students. Students learn the computer keyboard, practice work processing skills, and learn how to use different software programs. As part of this course, students also learn how to format business letters, resumes, and reports.

People who are drawn to high school teaching enjoy working with young people and enjoy the social activities that make up life in a high school. Teachers work five class periods a day, have a free lunch and conference period, and have a supervisory or tutorial session as a sixth assignment. Teaching is a very demanding profession. Teachers must help students master content and develop skills, maintain order in the classroom, help students with emotional and academic problems, meet with parents, provide information for staffings, produce parent notices, grade work, develop the curriculum, and evaluate student progress. In recognition of the demands that the profession makes on teachers, schools typically offer several breaks a year and an extended, but unpaid, vacation during the summer.

At a minimum, keyboarding teachers need a bachelor's degree in education with a minor in technology, or a bachelor's degree in vocational education combined with a teaching certificate to qualify for a job. These credentials will take roughly four years to earn while studying at an accredited college or university. Successful teachers have strong communication and interpersonal skills, enjoy working with young people, and are extremely organized. In a typical workday, a high school teacher may work with 150 students, all of whom need instruction and attention.

Demand for keyboarding teachers will grow as teachers retire and as school districts expand their offerings in technology. In many school districts, keyboarding proficiency has become a high school graduation requirement. The salary schedule for all teachers depends on salary schedules that each school district in the United States and Canada determines, so salaries vary widely. In general, the national average for high school teachers is $34,000.

CHAPTER 2

TEACHING TECHNOLOGY IN COLLEGE

COLLEGE INSTRUCTOR IN TECHNOLOGY

Dr. Urban Thobe is the dean of the Department of Technology at Oakton College in Des Plaines, Illinois.

What education and technical background is most helpful to aspiring candidates in this field?

The basic state guideline in Illinois is that instructors must have at least two thousand hours of experience in the field that they are teaching. That guideline comes as a shock to some people, but remember that there are no college degrees in many of the occupational fields, like welding, for example. At Oakton we expect division chairs to have a minimum of a bachelor's degree, and many of our chairs have master's degrees in engineering. We expect all of our full-time staff to have a bachelor's degree in some field, even though the field may not be a degree program in their area of teaching. When we hire part-time staff, we look for people who have completed some college courses; they need the experience of being a student before they can be a teacher.

What kind of experience should an aspiring candidate have?

The ideal candidate has a combination of work experience in his or her subject area and some kind of formal teaching experience. You can never tell who is going to be a good teacher by looking at a resume, but you can look for communication skills and evidence of the ability to deal with people effectively. I would say that the ideal candidate has a thorough knowledge of his or her subject matter and has extensive work experience that is appropriate to the subject to be taught. Applicants who have experience as adjunct teachers at a college have a significant advantage.

What advice would you give to someone who is interested in teaching at the college level?

This is very challenging work, but it is a very interesting field. We are not bound by all the bureaucracy that you find in high school, and we don't have the publishing and research commitments that you find in other departments at the college or university level. Our program is industry driven. We exist to train people for jobs in industry. In order to be successful, applicants must have technical skills that are in demand, and they must update and expand on those skills. Students know the job market better than anyone else, and we respond to student enrollment.

People who enter this field—especially division chairs—must be willing to look at their divisions as small businesses. They need to network with trade and industry associations to stay current with their field, and they need to work with schools and community associations to recruit students. All of the divisions work with advisory committees to keep their programs focused on industry. Unless the divisions develop courses that offer what students need, their programs will die.

Teaching opportunities in technology at the college level usually fall into three categories: adjunct faculty, full-time faculty, and division chairs.

Adjunct faculty are instructors who teach one or two courses in their specialty areas and are typically paid by the class. Adjunct faculty in technology must have a minimum of two thousand hours of experience in the field that they teach, and they need some kind of training or teaching experience, whether it is as a volunteer tutor or instructor of apprentices. At the very least, adjunct faculty should have earned some college credit so they will have an understanding of the needs and expectations of their students.

Adjunct faculty need to break the course content into activities and assignments that will allow students to learn the subject matter. They need to develop strong communication skills in order to present information, answer questions, and explain complex ideas. Adjunct faculty must develop appropriate tests and grading scales that measure student achievement in a fair and impartial manner.

In the classroom, adjunct faculty meet with students, explain assignments, answer questions, and present information. Adjunct faculty are responsible for creating and maintaining a safe and stimulating classroom environment. Adjunct faculty also administer tests and evaluate student progress.

Adjunct faculty are usually paid a set salary for each class that they teach. The hourly rate is usually quite attractive, but typically there are no fringe benefits and no job security for adjunct faculty. This is an excellent opportunity for people who enjoy not only teaching but careers in business and industry, and are not willing to give up these careers for full-time teaching.

Full-time faculty need a minimum of a bachelor's degree to qualify for a position, as well as two thousand hours of experience in the area that they will teach. Typically, full-time faculty are expected to bring a wide variety of experience in several teachable areas to the college or university, so they can teach a normal complement of five classes each semester. The teaching obligations are identical to adjunct faculty in terms of preparation and student contact, but full-time faculty are often expected to make contributions to departmental or college-level committees. As full-time staff, they enjoy job security, a salary that is determined either by a salary schedule or a negotiated contract, and a benefits package.

Division chairpeople share the same teaching responsibilities as adjunct faculty and full-time faculty, and they also have extensive additional responsibilities. Division chairs in technology are often described as academic entrepreneurs who must develop a keen insight into industry trends so they can develop and offer classes that students need. In order to stay current with new trends, division chairs read and research industry publications, develop advisory committees, and participate in industry organizations.

Division chairs recruit students for their programs and hire and evaluate faculty for their programs. Division chairs develop and administer a program budget and assist their staff with discipline and instructional problems.

People who are attracted to college-level teaching enjoy working with young people who are more focused and mature than high school students. College faculty enjoy focusing on teaching, as opposed to focusing on discipline and coaching obligations at the high school level, or on publication and research in other departments at the college and university level. College faculty enjoy an academic calendar that allows them a great deal of free time to spend with family or to use for continued education or projects.

Division chairs are paid on a salary schedule set by the college or negotiated by a professional organization. In general, salaries range from $41,000 to $55,000 a year.

Opportunities for college-level teachers of technology range widely. Qualified people who wish to teach as adjunct faculty are readily employable. Competition for full-time positions is much more intense, but many opportunities should develop as colleges expand their technology programs and as current faculty members retire.

CHAPTER 3

TEACHING TECHNOLOGY IN PROPRIETARY SCHOOLS

DIRECTOR

Roger Speer is the director of the Glendale Heights Campus of Universal Technical Institute in Glendale Heights, Illinois.

How would you describe a typical day at your job?

One of the reasons that I love this job is that there is no such thing as a typical day. I view this job as a kind of customer service position. I look at the staff members and students in this school as my customers, and I try to provide the kind of leadership the school needs. I am responsible for supervising instruction, staffing, student aid, and job placement at this school. Those are ongoing issues. I am also responsible for working with students and families when students run into trouble here. We never have discipline problems. Normally students who are still with us after the first nine weeks graduate from our school. But there are some students who have trouble adjusting to our program. We are preparing students to take jobs in industry, so we insist on the kind of grooming, punctuality, courtesy, and cooperation that industry demands. Industry operates a drug-free workplace, and so we have developed one of the toughest drug-testing policies of any postsecondary school in America. When students have problems in these areas, I get involved. Over 70 percent of our students graduate, but I also work with the students who are on probation for academic failure or for failure due to nonattendance.

I also work with staff members who want to continue their formal education. Our school provides tuition reimbursements to staff members who want to continue their college educations. I also help coordinate professional education for our teachers, so they can keep up with new developments in industry.

One of the things that I enjoy the most is the ability to work with vocational education. Our school has helped develop the electrical and automotive contests for VICA [Vocational Instruction Clubs of America], and we are helping Gage Park High School develop a career academy. We are helping to provide technical assistance, curriculum materials, equipment, and teacher training opportunities for the academy.

I am also very interested in job placement for our students. Our goal is to match student ability with employer expectations. The first job a student gets is absolutely critical in determining the student's success. A bad entry-level experience can turn a student off to the whole field. We work hard to help employers read and evaluate our students' transcripts. Our transcripts have a tremendous amount of information in them: they contain student grades for academic work and labs and information on punctuality, courtesy, dependability, cooperation, intuition, attendance, and safety. Unfortunately, all the information in the world won't help an employer if he or she can't read and evaluate the transcript properly.

What experience or education was most helpful to you in preparing for your career?

I had a lot of experiences that helped me. I joined the Marine Corps right out of high school and became a sergeant. After the military, I worked in the oil fields as a crew chief on a gas rig. When I decided to go to college, I majored in business and entered the airline industry. I specialized in human resources, but when I came to UTI, I was fascinated by the education that was going on here. Kids light up when they get here. Maybe they had algebra in high school, but when they learn algebra in terms of Ohm's law, it makes sense to them. The chance to work with kids who are focused on their goals really appealed to me.

One of the projects that helped me prepare for this job was developing partnership programs with industry. We have partnerships with Firestone, BMW, and many other companies. These partnerships help us provide state-of-the-art equipment for our students, and they help us provide the kind of training that employers want. There is a kind of synergy here: the more up-to-date equipment, the better opportunities and the more job-specific skills that are developed. That's important for us. Professional technicians face complex challenges. They need critical-thinking skills, problem-solving skills, technical skills, and professional skills. The partnership program helps us to develop these skills.

What kind of background are you looking for in teachers who want to work with UTI?

We need teachers with a strong professional background. We want people who have done the jobs that they are training students to do. We also look for people who like kids and enjoy working with them. When we find a person who we think has the right background and the right personality, we are willing to invest the time and effort to train him or her. Prospective teachers actually sit in the class with other students and do the same lab work that the students do. We train prospective teachers to use our curriculum, to communicate, and to grade student work. But there are some things that you can't teach. Caring about students is one. Willingness to continue professional education, to keep learning in order to stay current with new developments in industry, is another. Those are qualities that you have to look for in people.

The director of a vocational proprietary school has many of the same responsibilities that a corporate manager and a high school principal have. Vocational school directors describe their major responsibilities as supervision, staffing, recruitment, and job placement.

School directors work with students who have difficulty with academic or discipline problems. The school director acts as a hearing officer for students who wish to appeal a decision made at a lower level. The director also works with the parents of students who are involved in problems at school. In their capacity as managers, school directors must also work with staff members who may be having personal or professional problems. When remediation plans fail, the director may need to make the painful decision to expel a student or to dismiss a staff member.

School directors are also deeply involved in all staffing decisions and usually are required to make the final selection from a pool of candidates that have been screened by the personnel office or by staff committee. The director works with staff to implement school improvement plans based on feedback from students, staff members, employers, and advisory groups. The director coordinates continuing education for teachers who need to learn about new developments in technology.

One of the most important aspects of a vocational school director's job is to coordinate student recruitment and job placement. Since proprietary schools are self-supporting, recruitment of new students is critical. In large measure, recruitment depends on how successful the school is in placing their graduates in jobs. The director supervises recruitment and placement counselors and works to develop partnerships with secondary schools and with industry to attract students and to offer training that will lead to employment.

School directors have a very demanding job. Personnel and student issues can be very time consuming and emotionally draining. Successful school directors thrive on the excitement of working with young people and enjoy the challenges of running a rigorous and economically viable school. Directors tend to work very long hours in meetings and in one-on-one conferences with students and staff. Volunteer work with professional organizations also consumes a great deal of time. Since proprietary schools do not follow a traditional school calendar, school directors can not look forward to a relatively peaceful summer break.

People who are interested in this field will require a strong background in business and education. A minimum of a bachelor's degree in business is required, and many schools require advanced work in management and in education. Competition for school directorships is very keen, partly because it's a very challenging job, and because the salary reflects those challenges. Vocational school directors earn between $70,000 and $100,000 a year.

Successful candidates in this field will have strong professional and academic backgrounds and impressive communications skills. There will be some growth in this field as new schools open and as currently employed school directors retire.

DEAN OF ACADEMIC AFFAIRS

Pat Kapper is the dean of academic affairs at DeVry Institute of Technology.

What kind of academic and work experiences did the most to prepare you for your role as a department chair?

The best training experiences I had were leadership opportunities in professional organizations. For example, I was the national vice president of the American Vocational Association, and I learned a great deal from my experiences in the association. I think that co-curricular activities in college can also be very helpful. I always encourage students to work in professional organizations because employers look beyond grades and transcripts. They want to hire employees who can handle multiple priorities. Successful students who are active in organizations and still earn good grades demonstrate that they can do several things at the same time, and do them well.

How did you become interested in school administration?

I happened into it. My boss was taking a medical leave of absence, and they needed someone to take over her responsibilities for a short period of time. As it turned out, she never returned, and I continued on as an administrator. It was not a conscious decision. I really enjoyed teaching, but I felt that I really needed to help out in an emergency. The longer I stayed in the job, the more I felt that I was broadening my skills as an administrator.

What kind of preparation would you recommend for someone who is interested in school administration?

There are certain skills that administrators simply must learn. The most important set of skills that I would suggest developing is people skills. The ability to get along with other people is absolutely critical. In descending order, I would add leadership skills and written communication skills. When our advisory board members ask alumni to talk to our students about ways to improve their education, the overwhelming response is to work in oral and written communication skills.

How would you describe a typical workday? What kinds of activities tend to dominate your day?

Usually several things are going on at the same time. I spend a lot of time developing the academic budget and on day-to-day management issues. I also supervise a large staff of people, so there are supervisory and people issues that come up. I enjoy working with the school curriculum, even though it can be very time-consuming. In order for us to do a good job, we need to make sure that our curriculum matches the needs that business and industry have. I spend a lot of time with division heads to discuss our academic program and make changes as needed. I meet with faculty, and I meet with students who need advice on their academic careers. Sometimes I need to meet with students who are not going to be successful in school, and I have to counsel them to look for other options.

When you are hiring new staff, what particular qualities do you look for?

We look for people who have actually done the job that they are preparing students to do. We want people with real-life experiences and teaching skills. We are not interested in people with research backgrounds. All of our faculty have a minimum of a master's degree in their field, and the best candidates have a teaching background either as a teacher in an evening program or as a teaching assistant in college.

What recommendations would you make to a potential candidate?

Obviously you will need to have the credentials that we are looking for. We get between one hundred and one hundred and fifty resumes for every teaching position that we advertise, and you would be surprised by how many people apply for jobs that they simply are not qualified for. Unless you meet the minimum requirements in terms of education and experience, you will not be interviewed. The next suggestion I would make is to be extremely careful with your resume. When a school gets the volume of resumes that we do, resumes that are handwritten or sloppy or contain spelling or grammar errors are seldom considered. I would also suggest that potential candidates practice interviewing before they come in for the real thing. We always do mock interviews with our students as part of their career development course, and then the students interview with members of our advisory board. They can use the feedback they receive to work on problems with their resume.

Candidates should arrive early enough so that they can try to relax and collect their thoughts before the interview begins. They should be careful not to smoke before or during the interview. They should never place their resume or notes on the interviewer's desk. It's important to respect the interviewer's space. Probably the best suggestion that I could give is to prepare questions to ask the interviewer, such as what kinds of skills and qualities are important to the company. Appropriate questions give the applicant a chance to pattern his or her responses to what the interviewer needs to hear. I would also say that applicants need to take the time to listen to the questions and think about answers. No one expects applicants to rattle off answers instantly. People need time to organize their thoughts. Applicants should also be willing to expand on their answers and go beyond "yes" or "no" answers. They need to watch the interviewer's body language to get a sense of when they should stop. These are skills that only come with practice, and that is why the mock interview is such an important tool.

When asked about the most demanding and time-consuming part of their jobs, deans of academic affairs all describe the problem of dealing with people under stress, whether it involves hiring staff, supervising and evaluating staff, advising students, or planning and implementing budgets. As challenging as this is, human relations comprise only one part of the dean's job. Deans are expected to develop and administer budgets, hire and supervise staff, develop and revise the curriculum, and advise students. This is difficult, demanding work.

People who are drawn to administration generally enjoy the challenge of shaping programs to meet student needs. They often have definite ideas about how an ideal school should work and derive great satisfaction from the day-to-day decisions that bring the school closer to their dream. This is challenging work. Deans deal with conflict, invest time in meetings, and are confronted with the minutia of making a school run. At the same time, deans must become experts in the academic areas under their supervision and careful evaluators of the faculty that they supervise. Deans hold a responsible and respected position in the academic community and command the commensurate salary and benefits. Average salaries for academic deans range from $70,000 to $90,000 a year.

In order to qualify for this position, applicants must earn a master's degree, and in many cases schools will require a Ph.D. In addition to the academic credentials, academic deans need to develop excellent communication and human relations skills. They particularly need to learn how to deal with students and faculty who may be under stress. The need to plan for long-term goals while meeting the day-to-day obligations of their job requires tremendous organizational skills.

Because of the limited number of administrators most schools require, opportunities for academic deans will continue to be very limited. Most opportunities in this field will occur as currently employed deans retire.

TECHNOLOGY INSTRUCTOR

Keith Geils is an instructor of heating, ventilating, air-conditioning, and refrigeration (HVAC) at Universal Technical Institute.

How did you become interested in teaching technology?

I started teaching when I was in the army. I learned HVAC in the army and then I became an instructor. I liked teaching. After the service I went into industry. I spent thirty years in the field. I became the national service manager for Air Distribution Association Corporation. I enjoyed my career in industry, but when I decided that I wanted a career that did not involve constant travel, teaching was a natural choice for me.

What kind of preparation would you recommend for people who are interested in teaching at a vocational school?

I would recommend a combination of formal education and field experience. College-level education is very helpful, especially when you teach the applied physics part of the course. Heating and air-conditioning is becoming very complex. You can't approach the job with a tool box in the back of a pickup truck anymore. A bachelor's degree in technology helps give you the theoretical background that you need for the job. But people who teach here need field experience, too. You need to know what it like to do the job yourself before you can teach anybody else. If you made a living in this field, if you had your own business, then you know what a student needs to accomplish to become a good employee.

When I grade students, I look at them as if they were my employees. I look at their dedication, attitudes, professionalism, as well as skills. My goal is to help kids learn the life skills that they need—things like appearance, behavior, punctuality—that will help them get jobs and become successful in their careers. If I didn't have a background in industry, I wouldn't know how to get these young people ready for a job.

What do you enjoy most about your career?

I love to watch kids grow up. If you don't enjoy kids, teaching is not much fun.

How would you describe teaching at UTI?

I love teaching here because I get to work with young folks who are focused on their goals. This is an interesting place to work because we get a core curriculum that we need to cover, but we can enrich that curriculum with additional labs for students who want to learn more. We have a ninety-hour block of time spread out over three weeks for each course. Students take one course at a time, so they can concentrate. The class breaks down into a theoretical phase, where we teach applied physics, and a lab phase. Teaching the theoretical phase can be difficult. The information is complex, and you've got to be able to tell the same story seven different ways. When we move over to the lab phase, the students need to master several kinds of equipment as well as split systems, which are the kinds of systems found in most houses, and package systems, which are the types of systems used in industry—both standard efficiency and high-efficiency versions.

Lab work gives students a lot of opportunities to demonstrate their own initiative. Students who master the core curriculum can move ahead to advanced projects, so you never have any bored students sitting around. If they make a mistake on a project and break something, they get to fix it, which is a good learning experience in and of itself.

Do you have any advice for someone who might be interested in entering this field?

People who teach in this field should know that they will have to go back to school to keep up with new developments in technology. As industry changes refrigerants and new system controls are developed, we will all have to learn new techniques, so our students can take advantage of the huge number of job opportunities these changes will produce.

TECHNOLOGY INSTRUCTOR

Michael Woods is a diesel engine and power train instructor at Universal Technical Institute.

How would you describe a typical day in your classroom?

Right now my class is working on labs. I describe what the class is going to do. I describe the project and tell the class what I expect from them. I assign groups and we start the lab.

The labs are all based on an engine or power train problem. The students need to follow a standard procedure for discovering what the problem is, taking the engine or power train apart, and making the repair. Their whole purpose is to confirm their diagnosis. Students work in groups of two or three, and the project is designed to include checkpoints where the students stop work, and I come over to check their work and authorize them to continue.

When I work with students, I explain that I have two roles. During the lab I am their supervisor, but at the end of the lab, I take on the role of their customer. They need to learn how to explain what they did and why they did it in terms that a customer is going to understand. If you can successfully explain something in simple terms to someone who does not understand the procedures involved, then you know what you are doing.

What do you like best about teaching at UTI?

The students really want to succeed. I can run a class that's pretty close to a shop situation. The only difference is that I've got thirty apprentices to work with. The students all have to master certain tasks, but if you want to increase their range, you have the freedom to expand the curriculum with more advanced labs. Kids can learn at their own pace, without anyone being held back. That's very important to us, because students can't move on to another project until they have mastered the skills they need. I like the challenge of making this work, because I know from my own experience that this vocation desperately needs good technicians.

What advice would you give to a new teacher in this field?

A lot of new teachers expect students to have more background information than they do. It's important to understand what kinds of skills students bring to class. Many students are interested in technology, but they come from high schools that have no technology programs, and they don't have a lot of background or many skills yet. New teachers must be willing to simplify explanations and make students demonstrate that they actually know what they're doing before they move on.

Technology teachers have many responsibilities. They present information on electrical, engineering, computer, refrigeration, or automotive theory so students can understand how their specialized field works. Then they design and supervise laboratory activities that allow students to put theory into practice.

Labs must be carefully supervised to ensure student safety and to allow teachers specific times to check on their students' progress before the students can continue with their work. Many proprietary schools develop special projects that students can use at the beginning of their lab experience, but teachers must create more advanced projects for students to work on and more challenging problems for them to solve. In proprietary schools, students tend to work at their own pace, so teachers must be willing to work with students who have very different ability levels.

Technology teachers work with students who need remedial help, and they spend a great deal of their time evaluating the students' progress. In many schools, students are graded on theory, lab work, attitude, initatitive, punctuality, and attendance. Placing numerical or letter grades on some of these subjective areas is extremely challenging and time-consuming.

Teachers in technical schools do not follow a traditional school calendar. Vocational schools are usually open fifty to fifty-one weeks a year. Teachers generally are given a set vacation package and may earn more vacation days as they increase their seniority. In many technical schools, teachers have access to a predesigned curriculum that covers the minimum requirements for the class. Teachers are expected to add activities and lessons both for students who need extra help and for students who need more challenging material.

Working conditions in proprietary school are generally excellent. Many schools also provide outstanding health and benefit packages. When asked what they enjoy most about working in a proprietary school, teachers generally comment on how much they enjoy working with students who are focused on their careers. Teachers also point out that there are no discipline problems in proprietary schools and that teachers are not required to coach or sponsor co-curricular activities.

Many proprietary schools will provide their staff with extensive teacher training, but successful applicants must have a minimum of three to five years of on-the-job experience in their area of specialty before they will be considered for a teaching position. Successful candidates will also have some formal postsecondary education at a college or university to complement their work experience. In order to be a successful teacher, candidates must have strong communication skills and great patience in dealing with students at all skill levels. Successful teachers are extremely organized and are not stressed by the challenges of running labs that involve many groups of students working on many different projects. In most proprietary schools, teachers are evaluated by their students; successful teachers are not threatened by this process and are willing to look at the information and adjust their teaching style as necessary.

Salaries in proprietary technical schools vary from school to school but tend to be competitive with public high schools. Beginning teachers in proprietary schools earn between $28,000 and $30,000 a year.

Opportunities in this field will continue to grow as proprietary schools expand to meet a growing school-age population and as currently employed teachers retire.

PROFESSOR

Linda Hjorth is a professor of clinical psychology at DeVry Institute.

What made you interested in teaching at a proprietary school as opposed to a public institution?

I grew up in a family of engineers, so I suppose I have always been interested in that area. I was very interested in psychology, but I wanted to teach in a professional atmosphere. I wanted to work with students who genuinely wanted to learn.

What are some special challenges that teachers in proprietary schools face?

Because I teach classes in psychology, career development, and social issues in technology, students sometimes think that my classes are not important and that they shouldn't have to work as hard as I push them. I hear things like, "Why do I have to take a class that is harder than my technical classes?" I think that part of the problem is that my classes deal with abstract issues, and most of the students are at DeVry because they love concrete, hands-on kinds of experiences.

How would you describe a typical day as a professor at DeVry?

I spend a lot of time preparing lesson plans for my classes. I research and write lectures, meet with students, teach classes, and grade a tremendous number of papers.

What advice would you give to someone who is interested in teaching at a proprietary school?

The most important suggestion that I could make is to get teacher training experiences. People who move from industry to teaching sometimes have a very difficult transition from executive to professor. People who are interested in this field should be prepared for a twelve-month teaching year and a variety of classes during the year. New people in this field need to spend a great deal of time and effort working on the projects and activities that they want their students to do, and they need to develop careful instructions for their students, so students know what is expected of them. The students we see at DeVry take their education very seriously, and they want to know what professors expect of them.

Educators who choose careers in proprietary schools are attracted by the opportunity to work with students who are focused on careers and who will work to attain the skills and knowledge that they need to succeed in their careers. Proprietary schools also offer other opportunities to educators. While professors at colleges and universities may feel the pressure to do research and to publish, and teachers in secondary schools may feel compelled to assume many responsibilities for co-curricular activities, professors at proprietary schools are free to focus on their teaching. Typically professors in proprietary schools do not face the discipline issues that occur in high school or undergraduate classrooms. Teachers who are frustrated by tenure laws that seem to protect slipshod professionals enjoy working in an atmosphere that demands a high level of professional commitment.

Professors who teach in proprietary schools spend their time preparing classes, meeting with students, grading work, and participating in committee work at the department or school level. Professors enjoy a fairly flexible schedule and often are responsible for five or six classes each semester. Because proprietary schools must match their course content with current demands in business and industry, professors must invest a great deal of time upgrading their knowledge base. Classes may range from lectures in front of hundreds of students to seminars that are designed for fewer than thirty students. Each different teaching situation demands excellent communication skills. Professors must also spend time developing learning experiences that help students master the course material and must establish fair standards for assignment and course grades.

In order to qualify for consideration as a professor, applicants must have a strong background in the specialized field that they plan to teach. Typically proprietary schools look for faculty who have held the job that they will prepare other people to qualify for. In addition to the required business or industrial background, applicants must have a master's degree in their field and must have demonstrated their skills as a communicator and a teacher. Many applicants are encouraged to teach evening school courses as a way to develop these skills. Since proprietary schools do not typically run on a traditional school year, applicants should be prepared for an extended school year.

Faculty at proprietary schools tend to be very happy with their careers. There is very little job turnover. The national average salary for educators at proprietary schools is $43,000 a year, but salaries may vary from school to school and department to department, depending on the school's specific needs.

CHAPTER 4

MEDIA AND INFORMATION CAREERS IN EDUCATION

COMPUTER COORDINATOR

Jeff Thieman is the computer services coordinator at Rolling Meadows High School in Rolling Meadows, Illinois.

How would you describe a typical workday? What kinds of activities tend to dominate your workday?

Certain activities occur daily, such as booting up the lab in the morning, supervising the lab when the aide is out on an errand, fielding phone calls from "lost sheep," and being the "Shell Answer Man" for any computer problem. Aside from teaching two periods a day, other activities range from solving computer hardware/software problems at my desk and in the field, to recovering lost/damaged files from a student's disk, to processing software requests, to managing the annual software supply budget, to making recommendations for the building's hardware budget. In this third, and last, year of our school district's technology push, the coordinator has recommended hardware for purchases of approximately one million dollars for one building. It wouldn't be surprising for the coordinator to walk in one morning with nothing to do for the day (this has never happened) and still be busy with all the "fires" that pop up. It is quite normal to go out on a call and fix one problem and then come back with three more problems to fix from people met on the way.

What long-range problems should people who work with computers in school be concerned about?

Networking, security, and integration of the curriculum on-line. The Internet will be a hot, controversial topic to be considered.

What academic preparation did you have for this job?

I have a math degree and in college I took a few computer programming courses. Aside from possessing a logical, problem-solving mind and on-the-job experience, there is no academic course work that could prepare someone for this job.

If you were going to give advice to someone who is interested in a career as a computer coordinator in a high school, what would you say?

Don't overestimate the knowledge base of the general public you're working with. Most of them don't know what they want or need, and their questions regarding problems are usually worded in the wrong way. People skills are a must, and you must learn how to say "no" to many requests. By not saying "no" your workload will increase exponentially until you go screaming into the night. Usually the people who ask for a lot of help and receive it will only make larger requests that will usurp your entire day.

What is the most challenging part of your day?

Staying up with the technology as it changes on an almost daily basis. People expect you to have an immediate answer to their problem. Unless you have spent hours doing what they are doing now, you won't be able to address their problem. Also, teaching two classes a day breaks the day into fragments that are oftentimes too short to afford tackling a project.

What is the most rewarding part of your job?

Solving the longtime nagging software/hardware problem. The flexibility in the schedule of the day is nice. Knowing that you can help people with their problems is also rewarding.

If you could change career paths, would you still choose a career as a computer coordinator?

This is a position that you grow into rather than prepare for. It's virtually impossible to anticipate whether you will like this position or not. There are days when things go very slick and everything works out. By the same token, there are days in which you take one step forward and three steps back. Those days provide you with the next day's agenda. I'm not sure that I would go into this field again. Teaching five math classes a day is much less of a headache.

One of the newest developments in education is the introduction of computers in classrooms, libraries, and computer labs. The process of selecting computer hardware and software requires tremendous technical expertise, and once the hardware is installed, schools need trained staff members who can maintain the computers, teach students and staff how to use computers and computer software effectively, and help teachers integrate this new technology into their curriculum.

Computer service coordinators assume many of these responsibilities. They teach one or two academic classes, they plan and administer a technology budget with funds to buy new software and equipment, and they maintain the computers that are already on hand. Computer coordinators invest a great deal of time keeping up with new developments in technology so they can help their colleagues make informed decisions about purchasing new equipment and software.

Perhaps the most demanding part of the computer coordinator's job is the ongoing process of helping teachers and students use new technology. Computer coordinators describe their workdays as being filled with "emergencies," as they try to help staff members work with products that they don't really understand, including retrieving lost data, dealing with crashed hard drives, equipment failures, and software problems.

Many computer coordinators report that they feel torn between the excitement of working with new technology and the frustration of dealing with a demanding and unsophisticated public. "People expect us to have a magic button that will solve all of their programming problems," one coordinator observed. "When we explain that we can't undo some of their mistakes, they are furious with us." But in spite of the frustrations that are part of the job, computer coordinators generally enjoy their work. Computer coordinators are generally paid on the same salary schedule as teachers and are given a salary increment to compensate them for the extra time and effort they invest in the school. As tenured teachers, computer coordinators enjoy a great deal of job security, a benefits package, and all of the usual school holidays. Although they certainly have a very hectic schedule, computer coordinators do enjoy clean and safe working conditions in schools.

In order to prepare for a career as a computer coordinator, prospective applicants must earn a bachelor's degree in education and receive a teaching certificate from an accredited college or university. In order to develop an understanding of the special needs that teachers and students have, most computer coordinators spend several years as classroom teachers.

Effective computer coordinators are people who enjoy working with students and who are comfortable dealing with crisis situations. Computer coordinators typically develop excellent listening and communication skills, and they often develop the patience to deal with people who cannot express what they mean. One characteristic of all computer coordinators seems to be great organizational skill. In general, computer coordinators are able to juggle long-term and short-term projects successfully.

Opportunities for computer coordinators will continue to increase as schools expand their equipment and course offerings.

The general aging of the teaching population and the increase in teacher retirements will also create career opportunities.

MEDIA SERVICES DIRECTOR

Paul McDonough is the media services director for Rolling Meadows High School in Rolling Meadows, Illinois.

How would you describe a typical day in your job? What kinds of activities tend to dominate your workday?

I am not sure that I have a typical workday. I am never sure when someone will have an emergency, or when something will break down. My top priority is to make sure that teachers have the materials they need, and I help them when the equipment or software doesn't work. I enjoy spending part of my time showing teachers new materials that I think they will be able to use in the classroom to enhance their teaching.

How did you become interested in media services?

At the beginning of my teaching career, I noticed that students responded well to audiovisual materials. I have been promoting the use of audiovisual materials since 1970.

If you were going to give some advice to someone who is interested in a career in media services, what would you say?

In order to qualify for this job, a candidate must become a certified teacher, teach for several years, and then get a master's degree in audiovisual media. The teaching background is absolutely essential. People who try to jump into media services right out of graduate school do not understand student or teacher needs. I would say that the experience of graduate school makes a lot more sense for someone who has the concrete teaching experience to apply to the ideas that are being presented there. Successful media services people also have a strong background in computers and some knowledge of television production.

What kind of academic preparation or work experience was most helpful to you in your career?

The experience of teaching in a high school classroom was incredibly helpful to me. It gave me the background to understand the kinds of materials that are appropriate for high school students, and it gave me good insights into teacher needs.

What would you describe as the most challenging part of your job?

I would say that there are two main issues for me. The first issue is the difficulty of staying abreast of all the new developments in technology, all of the hardware kinds of products, and the need to stay abreast of all the new software that is developed each year. In order to make intelligent decisions about which software to buy, I need to spend a lot of time looking at new products. The second issue is the difficulty of dealing with teachers who are afraid of new technology and who don't realize the possible benefits that technology can bring to their students. New technology can be very intimidating, and no one likes to feel dumb, but the time and energy invested in learning CD-ROM, laser disk, and computer technology can make a tremendous difference in the kind of success students have in the classroom.

What would you describe as the most rewarding part of the job?

I really enjoy watching students and teachers work with products that make learning come alive. You can actually see the excitement in the faces of teachers and students when they create a project using technology that they never thought they would be able to do, or when they develop a project that turns out exactly the way they planned it.

If you could choose a different career path, would you choose media services again?

Definitely. This is a very exciting field to be in at this time.

Twenty years ago, a media services or A.V. director was the person who ordered films and filmstrips for the school and made sure the materials were delivered to the right classroom. Today, media services directors must understand copyright laws, be familiar with CD-ROM and laser disk technology, keep up with new materials that are released on CD-ROM and laser disk formats, maintain a library of videotapes, understand radio and television production, and be able to repair and maintain video and computer equipment. The explosion of information and information technology has transformed the media services director's job. Media services people now are seen as building experts in the field of instructional technology, and that change makes the job more interesting, but much more demanding.

Media services directors usually do not have teaching assignments, so they can spend most of their workday helping teachers with equipment and software. Much of their time is spent training teachers how to use new materials. In addition, media services directors also process requests for A.V. materials and equipment, which means that they must make deliveries, pick up materials, and safeguard against theft. In many high schools, student volunteers deliver materials to classrooms, and the media services director must supervise this group of students, too.

Media services directors are called upon to develop long-term plans for improving technology in their schools. Media services directors must also take responsibility for developing and administering the media budget.

Any job that requires public contact is challenging, and media services is no exception. Media services directors must deal with multiple—and sometimes conflicting—priorities within the building. Limited budgets make it impossible to keep everyone in a school happy, and media services directors must sometimes make unpopular decisions. The need to consider long-term trends in media equipment and technology, as well as dealing with short-term issues, can also be difficult.

In spite of these difficulties, media services directors really enjoy working with young people and exploring new technologies. Media services directors work on the same school calendar that teachers and students do, and so they enjoy school holidays and an extended summer vacation. The salary for media services directors varies from school district to school district in the United States and Canada, but in general, media services directors earn more than the average teacher salary of $34,000 per year.

In order to qualify for this job, potential applicants must earn a bachelor's degree in education from an accredited college or university and qualify for a teaching certificate. Applicants will also need to earn a master's degree in audiovisual media.

Successful media services directors have strong communication skills and enjoy working with young people. Typically, media services people are extremely organized, can deal with long-term and short-term projects at the same time, and are not unduly stressed by emergency projects that crop up suddenly.

Growth in this field will continue to be slow, despite a burgeoning school population, because of the specialized nature of the job. Most opportunities in media services will be the result of retirees.

COMPUTER LAB SUPERVISOR

Sherri Wilson is a computer lab supervisor at Rolling Meadows High School in Rolling Meadows, Illinois.

How did you become interested in technology?

I began my teaching career by teaching business education. I progressed from the typewriter to the computer.

Why did you decide to work in a high school?

I like the age group, and I had a secondary teaching certificate in my major. I have also taught preschool, fifth grade, and adult education.

How would you describe a typical workday? What kinds of activities tend to dominate your workday?

Most of my time is spent in helping students and teachers. I install new programs, resolve problems with computers, and help students retrieve lost files. I also take time to learn new software and help with new equipment, such as unpacking powerbooks. I also supervise the lab, making sure that no damage is done to the equipment, and I am responsible for checking out equipment that is loaned to students.

If someone asked you for your advice on how to run a computer lab effectively, what skills and qualities would you suggest that they try to develop?

I would suggest that they try to learn as many new software programs as possible. There is a tremendous amount of material on the market, and it seems to change daily. I would also suggest that computer room supervisors work on communication and interpersonal skills. It's so important to be patient with students. Teachers can also be extremely demanding. Computers and computer software are so complicated that some problems may not have an explanation that laypeople can understand, but teachers and students just look at you with an expression that seems to say, "You could fix this for me, if you really wanted to."

What is the most challenging part of your job?

The hardest days are the days when programs conflict and won't work, or when the computers bomb.

What class or experience was most helpful to you in supervising a high school computer lab?

My background in high school teaching was very helpful.

If you could change one part of your job, what would it be?

I am pretty much self-sufficient. I can do anything that I need to when it comes to dealing with computers. I miss working with kids in computer classes, getting to know them and getting a sense of what problems a student might have with hardware or software.

When you started this job was there one suggestion or piece of advice that you wish someone would have told you?

Wear good running shoes.

As schools continue to expand their use of computers for instruction and keyboarding skills, they are faced with the choice of placing one computer in each classroom or creating computer labs where groups of students can use the computers for word processing, writing, keyboarding, or researching information from CD-ROMs or the Internet. In many cases, classroom teachers are not familiar enough with computers or computer software to help students who are faced with a computer that doesn't work properly or with software that malfunctions. Computer room supervisors help individual students use computer software and perform routine maintenance on the machines. Because of their efforts, teachers can focus on the academic needs of their students.

In a typical school, a computer room supervisor will spend six or seven class periods working directly with students in a computer lab, with scheduled breaks and a lunch period off. Working with students for one class period after another can be exhausting work, but people who are drawn to this field usually enjoy working with young people and are comfortable with technology. Although this work can be taxing, computer room supervisors enjoy a number of school holidays and an extended summer vacation.

People who are interested in a career in this field will need a minimum of sixty hours of college, and they will need a background in computer technology, either as part of their education background or as part of their work experience. Many computer room supervisors hold college degrees in technology and have earned their teaching certificates. Successful computer room supervisors have developed strong interpersonal skills and can relate well to students while maintaining a secure, productive work environment in their lab. Effective supervisors work efficiently and are able to manage many different activities at once, anticipating student needs, maintaining order in the lab, and keeping students on task.

There are more than 111,000 public and private schools in the United States and Canada, and many of them are adding computer labs to take advantage of new technology. Although the rate of pay for educational support personnel is usually much lower than that for classroom teachers, computer room supervisors usually earn $10.00 an hour or more.

CHAPTER 5

TECHNOLOGY EDUCATION IN BUSINESS AND INDUSTRY

CORPORATE EDUCATION

Ed Bales is the director of external systems education at Motorola University in Schaumburg, Illinois.

What skills do you look for in prospective employees in corporate education?

Some areas do require specific skills in engineering and marketing, but industry is also concerned with generic skills, such as verbal skills, written communication skills, math and science literacy, responsibility, teamwork, collaborative effort, and problem-solving skills. I can't overstate how important these skills are. Motorola and many other corporations have moved to design teams that include sales and engineering experts as well as experts from many other areas. In order to make those teams work, the people on the teams need generic as well as specific engineering or marketing skills.

For example, the new telephone we are developing is only touched by human hands four times during the manufacturing process. What do all the employees do? They solve production problems. When there are problems, groups get to work deciding how to solve the problems both now and permanently.

What kind of credentials do people need for this career?

People need a two-year associate's degree at a minimum, and many specialists in areas like engineering need more advanced degrees. One of the most important developments in corporate education is the development of instructional design. This is not the same thing as curriculum design. Instructional designers look at the competencies that people need for specific jobs. They examine the duties and tasks that make up the job, then they analyze the tasks that are critical to the job. In general, 20 percent of the tasks in a job are responsible for 80 percent of the success of the job. Instructional designers look at the knowledge and skills that are needed for success in the job and the attitudes and attributes that are important for the job—attitudes like responsibility, openness to change, and willingness to be part of a team and engage in teamwork. Openness to change is a very important attribute because many corporations are committed to continuous improvement, which requires continuous education and continuous change.

For the next step, the instructional designers develop a job model; then they find exemplary performers in the area to find out what they do that makes them so effective in their jobs. Education is compressed experience. The instructional designers work with exemplary performers to condense the experience these performers have and package it in ways that other people can learn. The exemplary performers become the subject area experts for the instructional designers. Instructional designers meet with exemplary performers for two to three days to find out what the exemplary performers do to be so successful.

Exemplary performers know what they do, but they often cannot describe how they actually improve their performance. The instructional designers listen to them, learn what they do, and design a program for other employees. Their goal is to capture experience and package it in ways that will engage adult learners.

What is a typical workday like for people in corporate education?

There is no typical day in this profession. Every day is different. Every group that you work with will have different strengths and needs.

Professionals in this field need to be familiar with many different methods of communication. Adults are not interested in the classic teacher/presenter model. We do not use the term *teacher* because it is too reminiscent of "lecturer" or "expert." Fifty percent of the learning that happens in class happens because of the interaction of the people in class.

People who are interested in instructional design must learn how to motivate people, how to use aspiration instead of fear as a motivating tool. Instructional designers must be aware of the specific needs of adult learners and learn appropriate strategies to present material effectively. People who have been trained in a traditional setting may have trouble adjusting to this. Collaborative learning is a workplace norm, but in high school, it is called cheating. Memorization is useless in a field where information becomes dated in a short period of time. People in this field must be committed to continuous learning and continuous improvement.

Continuous improvement means continuous learning. As industry adopts this philosophy of continuous improvement, tremendous opportunities are created for people who are interested in teaching in a corporate setting. Opportunities will vary from corporation to corporation; some companies will prefer to work with generalists who bring in specialists for consultation as needed. Other companies develop comprehensive programs that employ specialists in several areas. Although job titles and job descriptions will vary, most teaching opportunities will be in manufacturing support, technical support, supervision, marketing and sales support, management development, and instructional design.

Manufacturing support offers a wide range of teaching opportunities for people who are interested in teaching in a corporate setting. Most teaching opportunities require a bachelor's degree in the subject area and extensive work experience in a specialized area, such as engineering, computer programming, electronics, or chemistry. Instructors may be asked to develop a course that will teach a specific skill or process, or they may be asked to teach materials that have been developed by instructional designers. As instructors, their primary responsibility is to help employees master skills and understand the ideas covered in their course. Instructors present information, answer questions, and evaluate student progress. Teaching in a corporate setting is very different from teaching in a school because instructors are not always the content matter experts in a corporate class, and, in fact, a major responsibility that instructors have is to facilitate ways for employees to share their expertise with other employees.

Educational qualifications for these opportunities will vary from company to company, but in general, the minimum educational requirement is a bachelor's degree in business. Instructors who specialize in engineering or other subjects will need a degree in their area of specialization. In some cases, a master's degree will be required. Instructors who teach in occupational areas will need extensive work experience in their field.

People who are interested in this career will need to develop strong written and oral communication skills and extensive organizational skills. As with all instructors, they need to develop the ability to break complex skills and activities down into assignments that can be learned in a sequence that makes sense for adult learners.

People who work in manufacturing support usually enjoy excellent working conditions. Staff members work with interested and motivated adults and are free to focus on teaching as opposed to discipline, co-curricular activities, or publication. While these positions may include a significant amount of travel, instructors in this field enjoy competitive salaries and benefits. Salaries vary from corporation to corporation but usually range from $24,000 to $71,000 a year. Opportunities for instructors in this field will continue to expand as corporations focus on continuous improvement and as professionals in this area reach retirement age.

Supervisory training focuses on specific management skills that supervisors need in their day-to-day work. Instructors develop courses that teach problem-solving skills, evaluation and supervisory skills, organizational skills such as developing agendas and running meetings, and negotiating skills. Instructors also develop courses that teach supervisors how to deal with legal and ethical issues that they may face on the job. These classes may be developed by the instructors themselves, or they may be developed by instructional designers.

Professionals in this field need a minimum of a bachelor's degree in business, must develop strong communication and organizational skills, and must have the ability to create courses that will meet specific objectives. People who are attracted to this field enjoy working with adult learners and enjoy excellent working conditions. This career may entail some travel, but the salaries are generally competitive, ranging from $24,000 to $71,000 a year, and are usually part of a complete salary and benefits package. Opportunities in this career will remain strong with new positions being created by industry and other opportunities occurring as currently employed staff retire.

People who enjoy working with adult learners find many teaching opportunities in marketing and sales training. This is a huge field that includes professionals who teach customers how to use the technology they have purchased, to professionals who train marketing and sales staff. In most situations, a bachelor's degree in business is the minimum academic credential required, and in all cases, individuals who work in this area need strong written and verbal communication skills and must be able to relate to adult learners. Many corporations have developed detailed curricula for specific skills that they need taught, as well as more general courses in providing customer service, organizing trade shows, giving presentations, developing proposals, writing reports, and dealing with customer complaints. In some cases, instructors need to work with managers and customers to develop their own course materials. As with all teachers, instructors need to be able to create course work that will enable students to learn skills and content, as well as facilitate discussion, present and explain information, and evaluate student progress.

Working with adult learners can be challenging, but it is also very stimulating since adult learners tend to be very focused and motivated. Working conditions for instructors in marketing and sales vary widely. In many corporations, instructors in marketing and sales are expected to do extensive amounts of travel as they serve customers and staff in various parts of the country. Salary and benefits packages vary from corporation to corporation but are generally competitive, ranging from $24,000 to $71,000 a year. Opportunities for instructors in marketing and sales are predicted to remain strong.

People who are interested can also work with management to improve skills in areas such as negotiation, problem-solving, planning, and analysis. Frequently these specialists will work with managers to help them focus on reorganization and change. Since this is a highly specialized field, it requires a combination of advanced education and an impressive resume of corporate experience. Many of the professionals who work in this field are self-employed consultants who develop the specialized seminars and programs that deal with current topics and then present these programs as needed.

In addition to education and experience, people who are interested in this field need to develop exceptional communication and organizational skills and must be willing to travel extensively. Opportunities are extremely limited, but people who are drawn to this field enjoy working with extremely intelligent and articulate people who are sharply focused on their goals. Salary will depend on the skill of the consultant and on the programs the consultant can develop and market. The salary range can be from very marginal to more than $180,000 a year.

One of the newest and most interesting opportunities for people who are interested in teaching adults is instructional design. Instructional designers work with managers and supervisors to determine the skills that individuals need to learn for a specific job, and then work with employees who are exceptionally skilled at what they do to develop a course that teaches these skills to other employees. This is unusual in terms of teaching, because the teacher is not the content expert. In order to qualify for this position, applicants will need to earn a master's degree in instructional design. Applicants will also need to develop exceptional communication and organizational skills and be able to relate well with adult learners. People who are drawn to this field are interested in teaching and designing courses. Working conditions are excellent, and instructional designers have the opportunity to work with extremely motivated and interested people. Salaries in this field are excellent, ranging from $40,000 to $70,000 a year.

CHAPTER 6

STUDENT TEACHING

For professionals in technology education, one important step in the process of getting a job is to make effective use of student teaching. Everyone who aspires to work in secondary education will have to spend anywhere from nine to eighteen weeks working in a school under the direct supervision of a professional. Many students feel imposed upon by this requirement because they have to pay tuition to their college during the student teaching period, and they have to work forty hours a week without pay. Although this can be very frustrating, it is important to remember that the student teaching experience can become a nine- to eighteen-week audition for a job. Innovative, energetic, responsible student teachers can make a tremendous impression on colleagues and supervisors. The young people who complete teacher training experiences have a sense of what a school's goals and priorities are, and they have a sense of how the institution works. This insight makes them excellent candidates for a job. Personnel directors are comfortable hiring former student teachers because they can base their evaluation on an extended period of activity instead of relying on recommendations and a brief interview.

In order to make the best possible use of the student teaching experience, you need to plan in advance and you need to consider some very important questions:

What do you want to do? Secondary education is very challenging work. Before you decide to enter this field, you need to take stock of your strengths.

Have you mastered the material that you need to teach? Do you know the material so thoroughly that you can teach in spite of interruptions and distractions?

Do you have the patience to work with students who may not understand the material and who may need repetition?

Do you have the organizational skills necessary to create a structured environment for your students?

Can you create a classroom atmosphere that allows students to feel safe but demands that students strive for excellence?

Do you have the emotional stamina to work with young people who are faced with emotional upheavals?

Can you develop activities that will allow students to teach themselves by being engaged with meaningful work?

What are your long-term goals? Where do you want to be in five or ten years? What do you want to be doing in five or ten years?

Once you have taken stock of your strengths and interests and determined that secondary education appeals to you, you must consider a second, important question: where do you want to live?

Certification requirements vary from state to state in the United States, and almost as important, the school that you attend will have specific geographic boundaries for students who want to student teach. Colleges and universities simply cannot afford to send professors all over the country to supervise their students. If you are determined to live in a specific part of the country after you graduate from college, plan to attend college and perform your student teaching nearby. Appendixes A and B of this book list colleges and universities that offer degrees in technical education throughout the United States and Canada. Use these resources to help select a school in the part of the country where you want to spend your life. As you select your college or university, be sure to find out if you can pick the school at which you will perform your clinical experience. If so, you may be able to further your own career by selecting an institution that anticipates adding new staff in the immediate future.

OPPORTUNITIES

In order to find out which schools are expecting to add staff, you need to do some research. This project might sound a little overwhelming, but if you allow yourself a generous time line and break the task into three parts, it does not need to be terribly time-consuming.

1. Gather information.
2. Make an initial contact with the institution.
3. Write an introductory letter.

As you begin your junior year of college, start to gather information about schools that you might use for your student teaching. The schools should be in the geographical area that appeals to you, and must be within the boundaries that your college has set for sending supervising professors out for observation. There are several directories that will help you.

Private Independent Schools

Directory of Canadian Universities

Directory of Public Elementary and Secondary Education Agencies

Directory of Public School Systems in the United States

Once you are armed with the addresses and phone numbers of these schools, you need to sort through them and make a list of the schools that you might be interested in using for your student teaching experience. Pare the list down to a manageable size. Before you can write anyone and ask about opportunities for student teaching or future employment, you need to find out who you will be writing to. The process of calling personnel offices and asking who the personnel director is will take some time and cost some money, but it is an important step. Competent, professional people always know who they are writing to.

You can save some time and money if you plan out what you want to say before you dial. Ask for the personnel office. Explain that you are a student in the field of technical education and that you want to write the school and ask for some information. Find out how to spell the personnel director's name. Double check the spelling, his or her title, the mailing address, and the zip code.

Your next step is to draft an informal but professional-looking letter that asks for some information about the school district. Explain that you are a student in the area of technical education, and that as you are beginning to plan for your student teaching experience, you want to be sure that you are as well prepared as possible. Ask about the kinds of skills and qualifications that the personnel director thinks a successful professional should have. In a sentence or two describe why you want to work in special education, and discuss the kinds of experiences and training that you have. Be sure to ask the director's thoughts about a future in technical education and if the director anticipates any openings in the near future. An informal letter might look something like the letter on the next page.

Dr. Anne Gordon
High School District 275
1411 North Morningside Street
Elk Grove Village, Illinois 60008

Dear Dr. Gordon:

Like many students in technical education, I am a little
afraid that my course work is not enough preparation for my
student teaching experience. If it is not too much of an
imposition, I would like to call and ask you some questions
about the kinds of skills and qualifications you think a
successful teacher should have. I am beginning my junior
year at Northern Illinois University, in DeKalb, and
although I have enjoyed my course work and have had the
opportunity to volunteer as a teaching aide at de Tocqueville
High School, I want to look for opportunities that will give
me the skills that I need to do an excellent job. I would be
grateful for any insights that you have on preparation,
extracurricular activities, and opportunities for employment.

I know how busy you are, so I hope it will not be too great
an imposition if I call your secretary and find a time when I
could talk to you about these issues.

Sincerely,

Lucille Varga
403 South Market Street
DeKalb, Illinois 60160
(815) 555-0860

The content of the letter may be informal, but the format must be immaculate. Proofread carefully; make revisions as needed. This is the first impression that the personnel director will have of you. Misspellings, typos, and errors in grammar or syntax will work against you. Keep track of your responses, and when it is time to select a school for your clinical experience, be sure to pick the one that will offer you the best opportunities for education and employment.

THE VALUE OF EXPERIENCE

Many people have strong negative feelings about student teaching. Some people have concerns about covering tuition and living expenses while working at an unpaid job; other people are simply frightened of facing students in a real world situation. Try to get past these negative feelings. Student teaching can offer you a wide range of learning opportunities. The way you make use of this experience can help you find the job you want. When you are student teaching, be sure to ask the best teachers in your area if you can borrow and use lessons, unit plans, teaching strategies, and activities that they have developed. You may be able to adapt them for use later in your teaching career. Be sure to talk about situations and professional issues that concern you. Ask other professionals how they would deal with these concerns. The nine to eighteen weeks that you spend at that school can give you invaluable insights into your profession. If your student teaching experience offers the opportunity for committee work or coaching, be sure to take advantage of it. All of these activities will give you the opportunity to network with other professionals, establish a track record, and generate letters of recommendation from people who have actually seen you work. As you begin the process of applying for jobs, those recommendations will be extremely valuable to you.

Student teaching is unique to teachers in primary and secondary school, but anyone who wants to work in technical education will need to look for opportunities to get the kind of volunteer or work experience that builds a powerful resume.

One question dominates the whole process of finding a position in special education: "Why should we hire you instead of somebody else?"

Sometimes the question is asked out loud, sometimes it lingers in the air, sometimes it's only hinted at, but every successful applicant must be able to answer that question whether it's asked or not. And there is usually only one correct answer: "You should hire me because I have a proven track record of achievement in this field."

And the successful applicant must be able to cite specific accomplishments and experiences to back up that claim. The only way that young college graduates can obtain this experience is to make careful use of summer work, internships, and volunteer work.

SUMMER WORK, INTERNSHIPS, AND VOLUNTEER WORK

Summer work in business or industry can offer excellent opportunities to work in the field and to learn the language, attitudes, and corporate culture of the business. Summer work can also provide an opportunity to develop the kinds of interpersonal skills that you will need in your career. The best opportunities will allow you to use technology and to work with other people. Be sure to use this time to observe the ways in which other professionals work. Be sure to make note of ideas, strategies, and techniques that seem to be very effective.

If your work setting is fairly informal, you may be able to use your summer work as an opportunity to network with other professionals in your area. Every workplace has its own, often unwritten, rules about communication between permanent and temporary staff, but if you can find a professional who is willing to talk about serious issues in this field, you can network and learn a great deal at the same time.

At the end of your summer job, be sure to ask someone you respect to write you a letter of recommendation. Every letter of recommendation that you acquire helps to document your growth as a professional.

Internships are another way to gain valuable experience. Many students are reluctant to consider volunteering for an internship because they feel pressed by course loads or by the need to hold down a part-time job. However, a carefully selected internship can yield many benefits. Certainly the most tangible benefit is that anyone who reads your resume will know that you are committed to your career, and that you have the kind of self-discipline that allows you to trade free time for experience that will help you later in your career.

Another important benefit of internships is that you can choose the kind of experience that will help you the most. If you volunteer consistently, you can develop a network of professionals who can recommend you based on their observation of your performance. If you decide to volunteer for an internship, think about the kind of experience that you need to grow as a professional. Once you decide on the kind of experience that will help you, take a look at your schedule. You will need a short block of time that you can donate on a regular basis for a semester or for a school year. Once you know what you want to do and how much time you can give, check with your college placement office to see what opportunities exist. Since many companies use web sites to disseminate information, it would be wise to search the Internet to see if a company that you are interested in has a home page. Information on internships might be posted there. Another option is to contact the school or business that you are interested in and ask for the opportunity to volunteer.

Personnel directors are sometimes hesitant to accept volunteers. Confidentiality and liability are important considerations, and there is always the concern that volunteers may fail to follow through after they have been oriented and trained by the paid staff. In these cases, volunteers can actually be a drain on the organization's resources. You can allay a lot of these concerns by the way that you approach personnel directors. In general, you need to follow the same procedures that you used to select the school or facility for your student teaching or clinical experience. Select an organization. Find out the personnel director's or principal's name. Double check the spelling and address. Write a short letter that explains why you are interested in technology, what you are willing to do, how much time you can give, and how long you can continue to volunteer. Use a sentence or two to explain why you need a volunteer experience to enhance your own education. The administrator needs to know that you are volunteering because you want to be there, not because you have been sentenced to community service. Your letter might look something like the letter on the next page.

Dr. Gwen Schumacher
Principal, Alexis de Tocqueville School
2109 North First Street
DeKalb, Illinois 60160

Dear Dr. Schumacher:

As a sophomore technology major at Northern Illinois
University, I am concerned that the theories I am learning
will not make much sense unless I have a chance to work
with students. I need to see the connection between the skills
my professors talk about and the needs that students have. I
would be very interested in volunteering at the de Tocqueville
School as a technology center aide. My course schedule gives
me a two-hour block of time on Tuesdays and Thursdays
from 1:00 until 3:00 P.M. My schedule may change in
January, but I can be available every Tuesday and Thursday
from now until then.

I know that many schools are hesitant to use volunteers
because they sometimes fail to follow through on their
commitments. I understand their reluctance, but I can tell you
that I have been interested in special education since I was in
high school, and I view the opportunity to work with your
students and staff as an important learning experience. If you
accept me as a volunteer, I will live up to my commitment.

Sincerely,

Anup Shah
403 South Water Market
DeKalb, Illinois 60160

Once you begin your volunteer work, be punctual and show up when you are scheduled. Use this opportunity to work with staff. If your situation permits, talk with working professionals about issues in your field. This is an excellent opportunity to create a network of professional people whom you can turn to for advice, or who can provide valuable information about career opportunities. Before your volunteer experience ends, ask for a letter of recommendation from your supervisor or from someone with whom you have worked. Such a recommendation carries a great deal of weight and will help establish you as a competent, serious professional.

CHAPTER 7

RESUMES, APPLICATIONS, AND INTERVIEWS

RESUMES

The sole purpose of a resume is to get you an interview. If you have worked hard to get the experience and credentials that you need to build a winning resume, your next goal is to present that information effectively. Unfortunately, many people are so intimidated by the thought of "bragging" about themselves that they fail to provide potential employers with the information that might get them a job. Others are so worried about the format of the resume and the need to compress education and experience into a short, readable form that they delete important information just to make their credentials fit on one page. Before you start to work on your resume, take the time to answer a few questions:

1. What kind of job are you looking for?
2. Where do you want to work?
3. What work, internship, or volunteer experience do you have?
4. How does that experience relate to what you want to do?
5. What academic credentials do you have?
6. Is your school noted for its research or programs in technical education?

7. Does your school have the kind of prestige that makes a personnel director want to read your resume?
8. Have you achieved any special recognition for your studies or volunteer work?
9. Why do you want this particular job? What is it about this organization's philosophy, location, or salary that makes it special?

Once you have answered these questions, think about your strengths as a potential employee. As you develop your resume, you must emphasize these strengths. Many people are intimidated by the process of developing a resume, but the mechanics of a resume are very straightforward. There are five basic elements of a resume: heading, experience, education, honors and awards, and references.

Heading

This information includes your name, an address where you can always be reached, and a phone number for an answering machine or answering service.

Experience

You need to make one of your first important decisions here. If your strengths lie in experience, lead with it. If your strengths lie in your academic preparation, list that information first.

When you discuss your work experience, be careful to include jobs that directly relate to the job that you seek. Although resumes need to be brief, you shortchange yourself if you do not spend a sentence or two discussing the job responsibilities that relate to the job you want. A simple list of places where you worked and dates of employment may not be of much help. The personnel director who reads your resume needs to see a connection between the volunteer or work experience that you have had and the kinds of responsibilities that a new job might entail. If you are applying for a position in a secondary school, make sure that you include any coaching or extracurricular experience that you have acquired.

Education

All of the jobs that we have discussed require academic credentials, and many of these jobs also require a state license. Although it may not seem very logical, personnel directors receive resumes from people who apply for jobs but don't have the academic credentials to be hired for them. A personnel director must be able to scan your resume and find out what you are licensed to do. Be sure to include the name and address of the college or university that you attended and the dates you earned your degrees. List your licenses separately, and be sure that you include the date that you earned them.

In addition to your licenses and degrees, be sure to discuss any teachable minor areas of study. If you participated in any special activities in college, as a teaching assistant, peer tutor, or member of any college team, you need to include that information as well. The athletic, academic, and leadership skills that you developed through these activities can be very useful in any profession.

Honors and Awards

If you received a scholarship, or if you have been recognized for leadership or service, be sure to record that information on your resume. Even though the awards may not directly relate to your career goal, anything that demonstrates a willingness to assume responsibility or to provide leadership helps prospective employers see you as an asset to their organization.

Work on the rough draft of your resume. Don't be afraid to use more than one page. You need to provide specific information about your experience and credentials that will encourage a personnel director to call you for an interview. Don't delete important information just to keep your resume short.

There are several possible resume formats to choose from. Spend an hour or so looking at different formats and rearranging the information in them until you find a format that works for you. Please remember that the format is less important than careful attention to spelling, grammar, punctuation, and factual detail. It is important that you resist the temptation to embroider your resume with half truths or outright lies. Don't claim awards or experience that you don't have. Many personnel directors have excellent skills when it comes to reading body language. It is very likely that they will sense that something is wrong when they ask about credentials that you don't really have. Even if you are able to fabricate your way into a job, the stress of worrying about being exposed is not worth any advantage that a fraudulent resume can buy you.

References

If you have taken the time to ask for a recommendation from every one of the employers that you listed on your resume, copy the letters and attach them to your resume. If you have any letters pertaining to your volunteer experience, student teaching, clinical experience, or co-curricular activities, copy and attach those letters as well. You will also have a file of recommendations from professors and supervisors at your clinical experience. These letters will probably be confidential, so you must offer to have your placement file sent to the personnel director on request. The following sample resume might be a good starting point for your own efforts.

Elizabeth Cervantes
828 North Dunton Street
Arlington Heights, Illinois 60004
(708) 555-2036

Objective:	To teach students how to use technology.
Experience:	1992–1994. Alexis de Tocqueville School, 2901 North First Street, DeKalb, Illinois. I volunteered as a technology center aide at de Tocqueville School for two years. I worked in the technology center as an aide, and I worked as a tutor two afternoons a week.
	1993–1994. Precision Tool Company, 1529 Rand Road, Palatine, Illinois. I worked in the blueprint room from June until September in 1993 and 1994.
	1990–1994. Peer Tutor, Northern Illinois University, DeKalb, Illinois. I tutored students in reading and social sciences one afternoon a week for the four years that I was enrolled at Northern.
Education:	1990–1994. Northern Illinois University, DeKalb, Illinois. B.S. in Education, 1994.
Certification:	I am certified to teach technology and computer science.

Honors and Awards: Outstanding Senior Award, College of
Education, Northern Illinois University,
1994.

Outstanding Volunteer, 1994, de Tocqueville
High School, DeKalb, Illinois.

References: Dr. Gwen Schumacher, Principal, de
Tocqueville High School, 2901 North First
Street, DeKalb, Illinois.

Dr. Phillip Armbruster, Professor of
Education, Northern Illinois University,
DeKalb, Illinois.

Mr. Mark Thompson, Manager, Precision
Tool Company, 1529 Rand Road, Palatine,
Illinois.

COVER LETTER

In order to make the maximum impact, your resume must be accompanied by a cover letter that is addressed to the personnel director of the organization that you are applying to. The cover letter should explain why you want to work for that particular organization. The cover letter will be similar to the letter that you developed when you were surveying agencies for your clinical experience. Be sure to include any professional growth, such as conferences or programs that you have attended, and discuss any pertinent work experience that you think makes you a good candidate for the job. Proofread this letter carefully. This is not a time for poor spelling or sloppy grammar. The obvious disadvantage of writing a personalized letter to each personnel director is that it takes time, and job applicants often equate a careful job search with the total number of resumes sent out. Please remember that personnel directors are not looking for someone who needs a job; they are looking for someone who will fit their organization's particular needs and who wants to work in their particular organization. Careful research and personalized letters may be far more useful than any scattershot approach.

An appropriate cover letter might look something like the one on the following page.

Dr. Angela Martin
Assistant, Superintendent for Personnel
High School District 511
DeKalb, Illinois 62210

Dear Dr. Martin:

I was delighted when Dr. Gwen Schumacher of de
Tocqueville School suggested that there might be a job
opening this fall for a technology teacher at the Tilden High
School. My student teaching experience at de Tocqueville
was so challenging and satisfying that I would love to
continue my relationship with District 511 as a teacher. Over
the last several years, I have had the opportunity to observe
teachers and students at many schools, but the sense of
optimism, the level of caring, and the professionalism of the
staff in District 511 makes me want to be a part of that team. I
am enclosing my resume, and I hope that after you review my
volunteer and work experience, I will have the opportunity to
meet with you in an interview.

Sincerely,

Antonia Cano
321 Evergreen Street
Palatine, Illinois 60010
(847) 555-1837

THE PLACEMENT OFFICE

The first contact most students have with their college placement office or career center usually comes in the second semester of their senior year, when they are in the process of putting their placement files together. A college placement office will maintain a confidential file of student transcripts and recommendations, but that is only one of the many services that may be available. Placement offices may offer vocational interest inventories, career counseling, and aptitude tests. In most colleges the placement office is a clearinghouse for job information. Many schools produce newsletters with job listings as they come in. In order to derive the most benefit from your college placement office, be sure to start visiting the office early in your senior year. Find out what services are available, and get your credentials in order. If your school produces a mailing list of job listings, make sure that you subscribe to it.

APPLICATIONS

Typically a school district or other organization will send out a job application after receiving your resume and cover letter. Wading through a job application can be a very frustrating and time-consuming process, especially since the application always asks for the exact information that you spent hours organizing on your resume. Be patient. School districts, proprietary schools, universities, and corporations that employ licensed professionals are required to keep meticulous records. By using a standard employment application, they can keep track of hundreds of pieces of information and retrieve them when accrediting agencies want to inspect their records. As you type or print the information on your application, be sure that all of the information is accurate. Personnel directors will verify education and employment information, so be sure to include names, addresses, zip codes, and phone numbers.

EXPANDING THE JOB SEARCH IN SCHOOLS

While you follow up on job leads that are generated by your college's placement office or that you hear about through your network, be sure to expand your job search to the following directories for more information and possible leads to full- or part-time work.

Directory of Public Elementary and Secondary Education Agencies in the United States

Directory of Canadian Universities

Directory of Public School Systems in the United States

Education and Hiring Guide for Alaska, Hawaii, Idaho, Nevada, Montana, Oregon, Utah, Washington, and Wyoming

Patterson's American Education

Private Independent Schools

Private Schools in the United States

The Canadian Almanac and Directory

EXPANDING THE JOB SEARCH IN BUSINESS AND INDUSTRY

People who are interested in teaching technology in business and industry need to explore ways to gain on-the-job experience though internships or carefully planned summer employment.

There are several excellent sources of information on internships. Your university's placement office will have listings of internships, and there are a number of directories that list internships in technical fields. A few of the directories that may prove helpful are:

National Directory of Internships

Internships: Patterson's Guide

Student Guide to Mass Media Internships

New Careers Directory: Internships and Professional Opportunities in Social Change

The process of selecting and apply for an internship in business or industry is essentially the same as applying for volunteer experience in education. Your first step is to use the directories to research information about the possible internships. As you select possible sites, you will need to consider transportation and time commitments. You will also need to consider the kind of work experiences that will be most beneficial to you. Your next step is to find out the name of the personnel director for the business. Then compose a carefully written and carefully proofread letter that explains what you can offer the company and describes what you hope to learn from the internship.

Summer work is another valuable source of experience. There are several directories that can help you learn about companies in your field. Some print directories that can help you research your field are:

American Business Services Directory

America's Best Mid-Sized Companies

Advanced Marketing Technology

ACM/SIGGRAPH Education Directory

Corporate Media Directory

Corporate Training Directory

Corporate Technology Industry Association Membership Directory

Once you have used the print directories to identify companies in your field, look for companies that are in your geographic area. You may wish to research Internet directories to see if these companies have home pages or web sites that might provide additional information about internships or employment opportunities.

The Internet Directory

The Internet Yellow Pages

Internet World Yellow Pages

New Riders Official World Wide Web Yellow Pages

THE INTERVIEW

Preparing for the Interview

You send out resumes and cover letters, you send out applications and credentials files, you sift through letters of rejection, and you wait by the phone for someone, anyone, to call. Then, suddenly, the phone rings, and a polite person on the other end of the line asks when it would be convenient for you to stop by for an interview. After fifteen minutes of delirious joy your stomach begins to knot up. You are now face to face with the dreaded interview. For a few moments your mind races through every nightmarish mistake that you can possibly make during an interview. If possible, you are more frightened than before the phone rang.

Everyone is frightened by the prospect of a face-to-face interview, partly because we know that we have a lot at stake. Since the interview process is so time-consuming, personnel directors spend a great deal of energy sorting through the applications to prepare a short list of applicants to interview. The personal interview is probably the most crucial step in obtaining the job we want. So though it is normal to be anxious about the interview, it is important to invest that energy in preparing for the interview instead of torturing ourselves about it.

No matter what form the interview will take, the interviewer will be looking for some specific information about your skills, experience, and attitudes. The best way to prepare for an interview is to anticipate the kinds of questions the interviewer will ask. Expect questions on:

Academic Preparation: What are you licensed to do? What clients are you licensed to serve?

Experience: How has your volunteer experience, work experience, or student teaching experience prepared you to do the job that you are applying for? Think of specific examples of problems that you faced and solutions that you tried. Be prepared to talk about your successes and about the kinds of lessons that you learned from your failures. Think about specific skills and techniques that you learned in your training and experience, and be prepared to discuss them.

Attitudes: The interviewer will be very concerned about your attitudes toward work and toward other people. Most jobs in technical education require tremendous self-discipline. There is very little day-to-day supervision in this field. Supervisors have to trust their employees to live up to their professional obligations. The interviewer is looking for someone who is strongly self-directed, who is willing to invest personal time on professional growth, and who will ask for help when necessary, but who, in general, works independently. As you prepare for your interview, think of examples that can demonstrate this kind of self-motivated behavior.

The interviewer will also be very interested in your concern for other people and in your ability to work with young people and adults. Education is essentially a service industry. People in this field must be able to empathize, set limits, encourage change, and reward appropriate behavior. This career requires tolerance, compassion, and concern for young people. As you prepare for your interview, be sure to think about specific examples of this behavior.

Although it may not be asked out loud, the real question that you must answer is, "Why should we hire you instead of somebody else?" Think about that question, and be able to explain why your skills, experience, and attitudes make you the best possible choice for this job.

It's normal to be anxious about the interview, but remember that the people who will interview you have much at stake. For you the interview represents a few hours investment in time and stress, but the people who hire you are making a long-term commitment. In many cases they will have to live with their choice for the rest of their professional lives.

Behavior that might appear to be cold or condescending may actually just be fear. Most personnel directors are confident professionals who have developed an arsenal of questions that will give them the information that they need; but it is possible that a personnel director may be distracted by ill health or personal issues, or that the committee charged with conducting the interview may be so overwhelmed by the whole process of selecting staff, that they fail to ask the right questions, the questions that allow you to talk about your particular strengths. In order to deal with this situation, you need to make a short list of the points that you would like to make during your interview. If the interviewer fails to ask the right questions, be sure to bring the points up yourself. Include these points in your answers to other questions or near the end of the interview, when the interviewer asks if you have any questions or comments.

Conducting the Interview

After you have prepared for your interview, be sure to attend to a few important details.

Know Where You Are Going: You don't need the stress of consulting maps and asking for directions as the time for your interview draws nearer and nearer. If you are not absolutely certain of the location, make a point to drive past the place where the interview will be held before your appointment.

Be on Time: Plan to allow yourself fifteen minutes to go to the bathroom, freshen up, and relax before you start your interview.

Dress Professionally: Although many employees at schools and social service agencies dress casually, remember that they can afford to—they already have the job. Dress like a young professional in the business world. As a general rule of thumb, don't wear anything that will distract you from the questions that will be asked, such as shoes or ties that are too tight. Don't wear anything that will distract the interviewer from your answers.

Calm Down: Be calm, confident, and relaxed. You have taken the time to prepare for this interview. You have the list of the points that you want to make during the interview, and you are speaking to people who genuinely want you to be successful. You have done everything you can to ensure your success. Relax and enjoy the opportunity to talk to professionals in your field. No matter how the interview goes, you will have a valuable learning experience.

Listen: Take time to listen to the questions. Don't cut people off before they are finished speaking. Don't answer until you have a chance to think about what you are being asked. This is not a quiz show with the prize going to whomever hits the buzzer first. Take the time to listen carefully, understand what the interviewer wants, and phrase your answer. The interviewer has taken some time to think about what to ask, and it is perfectly reasonable to take your time with a carefully considered answer.

Follow-up: When the interview is over, be sure to telephone or write a short note thanking the personnel director for the opportunity to come in for an interview. The few minutes it takes to follow up on an interview are well invested. The follow-up note or phone call can be a second chance for you. The note you write or call you make can be a vehicle to mention any points that you overlooked during your interview. The small amount of extra effort required for a follow-up call or note also lets the personnel director know that you are genuinely interested in the job, that you are not just looking at the interview as a practice session.

AVOID THE EMOTIONAL ROLLER COASTER

Living through a job search is one of the most emotionally draining, frustrating events in anyone's life. It is very easy to look at every rejection letter and every interview as a referendum on your worth as a human being. Please remember that the interviewer or the interview committee is looking for a good job match. No one looks at an interview as an oral exam, with the job as a prize for the contestant who gets the most right answers. The goal is to find an applicant who has the skills that are needed, who can work with the existing staff, and who can bring a particular set of values and attitudes to the organization. Interviews are frustrating because the people who advertise the jobs and conduct the interviews may not be able to describe the exact qualities that they are looking for. It's impossible to do an accurate postmortem after the interview and determine just how well you have done, because you don't have all the information that you need. All you can do is prepare, answer the questions honestly, and then concentrate on the next application or the next interview.

UNIVERSITIES OFFERING A DEGREE IN BUSINESS AND EDUCATION

U.S. UNIVERSITIES

Alabama

Alabama A and M University
 P.O. Box 284
 Normal 35762

Alabama State University
 P.O. Box 271-915
 South Jackson Street
 Montgomery 36101-0271

Athens State College
 P.O. Box 2216
 Beaty Street
 Athens 36849

Auburn University
 Mary E. Martin Hall
 Auburn 36849

Jacksonville State University
 700 Pelham Road North
 Jacksonville 36265-9982

Tallemeda College
 637 West Battle Street
 Talladega 35160

Troy State University
 University Avenue
 Troy 36082

Tuskegee University
 Carnagie Hall
 Tuskegee 36088

University of Alabama
   Box 870132
   Tuscaloosa 35487-0132

University of Alabama-Birmingham
   University Station
   Birmingham 35294

University of Northern Alabama
   Wesleyan Avenue
   Florence 35632

University of Southern Alabama
   307 University Boulevard
   Mobile 36688

Arizona

Arizona State University
   Tempe 85287-0112

Grand Canyon University
   3300 West Camelback Road
   Phoenix 85017

Northern Arizona University
   Box 4084
   Flagstaff 86011

Arkansas

Arkansas State University
   P.O. Box 1630
   State University 72467

Harding University
   Box 762-Station A
   Searcy 72143

Henderson State University
   Arkadelphia 71923

John Brown University
   Siloam Springs 72761

Philander Smith College
   812 West Thirteenth Street
   Little Rock 72202

Southern Arkansas University
   Administration 222
   Fayetteville 72701

University of Arkansas-Monticello
  Monticello 71655

University of Arkansas-Pine Bluff
  1200 University Drive
  Pine Bluff 71601-2799

University of Central Arkansas
  Conway 72032

California

California State University-Stanislaus
  801 West Monte Vista Avenue
  Turlock 95380

California State University-Dominguez Hills
  Carson 90747

California State University-Fresno
  Shaw and Cedar Avenues
  Fresno 93740

California State University-Sacramento
  6000 J Street
  Sacramento 95819

Humboldt State University
  Arcata 95819

LaSierra University
  4700 Pierce Street
  Riverside 92515

San Diego State University
  5300 Campanile Drive
  San Diego 92182

San Francisco State University
  1600 Holloway Avenue
  San Francisco 94132

Southern California College
  55 Fair Drive
  Costa Mesa 92626

University of California-Irvine
  Irvine 92717

University of California-Riverside
  1100 Administration Building
  Riverside 92521

University of LaVerne
  1950 Third Street
  LaVerne 91750

University of the Pacific
  3601 Pacific Avenue
  Stockton 90608

Whittier College
  13406 East Philadelphia
  Whittier 90608

Colorado

Adams State College
  Alamosa 81102

University of Colorado-Boulder
  Campus Box B-7
  Boulder 80309

University of Colorado-Denver
  Campus Box 167-1200 Larimer
  Denver 80204

University of Northern Colorado
  Greeley 80639

Connecticut

Central Connecticut State University
  1615 Stanley Street
  New Britain 06050

Southern Connecticut State University
  501 Crescent Street
  New Haven 06515

University of Connecticut
  Storrs 06269

University of Hartford
  200 Bloomfield Avenue
  West Hartford 06117

Delaware

Delaware State College
  1200 North DuPont Highway
  Dover 19901

University of Delaware
116 Hullihen Hall
Newark 19716

District of Columbia

Trinity College
Michigan Avenue and Franklin Avenue NE
Washington, D.C. 20017

University of the District of Columbia
4200 Connecticut Avenue NW
Washington, D.C. 20008

Florida

Bethune-Cookman College
640 Second Avenue
Daytona Beach 32015

Edward Waters College
1659 Kings Road
Jacksonville 32209

Flagler College
P.O. Box 1027
St. Augustine 32085

Florida Atlantic University
P.O. Box 3091
Boca Raton 33431-0991

Florida International University
University Park
Miami 33199

Florida Southern College
111 Lake Hollingsworth Drive
Lakeland 33801

Florida State University
Tallahassee 32306

Jacksonville University
2800 University Boulevard
Jacksonville 32211

Palm Beach Atlantic College
1101 South Olive Avenue
West Palm Beach 33401

Saint Leo College
    P.O. Box 20008
    Saint Leo 33574

University of Central Florida
    P.O. Box 25000
    Orlando 32816

University of Miami
    P.O. Box 248025
    Coral Gables 33124

University of North Florida
    P.O. Box 17074
    Jacksonville 32216

University of South Florida
    4202 Fowler Avenue
    Tampa 33620

University of West Florida
    11000 University Parkway
    Pensacola 32514

Georgia

Albany State College
    504 College Drive
    Albany 31705

Armstrong State College
    11935 Abercorn Street
    Savannah 31419

Augusta College
    2500 Walton Way
    Augusta 30910

Columbus College
    Algonquin Drive-Richards Building
    Columbus 31993

Fort Valley State College
    805 State College Drive
    Fort Valley 31030

Georgia Southern University
    Box 8024
    Statesboro 30458

Georgia Southwestern
  Wheatley Street
  Americus 31709

Georgia State University
  University Plaza
  Atlanta 30303

Mercer University
  1400 Coleman Avenue
  Macon 31207

Morris Brown College
  643 Martin Luther King, Jr., Drive NW
  Atlanta 30314

North Georgia College
  Dahlonega 30597

Piedmont College
  Demorest 30535

University of Georgia
  114 Academic Building
  Athens 30602

Valdosta State College
  1500 North Patterson Street
  Valdosta 31698

West Georgia College
  Carrollton 30118

Idaho

Boise State University
  1910 University Drive
  Boise 83725

Idaho State University
  P.O. Box 8054
  Pocatello 83209

Lewis Clark State College
  Eighth Avenue and Sixth Street
  Lewiston 83501

University of Idaho
  Moscow 83843

Illinois

Barat College
    700 East Westleigh Road
    Lake Forest 60045

Blackburn College
    700 College Avenue
    Carlinville 62626

Bradley University
    1501 West Bradley
    Peoria 61625

Chicago State University
    Ninety-Fifth Street at King Drive
    Chicago 60628

Eastern Illinois University
    Old Main-Room 116
    Charleston 61920

Elmhurst College
    190 Prospect Avenue
    Elmhurst 60126-3296

Greenville College
    315 East College Avenue
    Greenville 62246

Illinois Benedictine College
    5700 College Road
    Lisle 60532

Illinois State University
    201 Hovey Hall
    Normal 61761

Lewis University
    Route 53
    Romeoville 60441

Loyola University of Chicago
    820 North Michigan Avenue
    Chicago 60611

MacMurry College
    447 East College Street
    Jacksonville 62650

Monmouth College
   700 East Broadway
   Monmouth 61462

National Lewis University
   2840 Sheridan Road
   Evanston 60201

Northeastern Illinois University
   5500 North St. Louis Avenue
   Chicago 60625

Northern Illinois University
   DeKalb 60115

Northwestern University
   P.O. Box 3060-1801 Hinman Avenue
   Evanston 60201-3060

Quincy University
   1800 College Avenue
   Quincy 62301

Southern Illinois University at Carbondale
   Woody Hall
   Carbondale 62901

Southern Illinois University at Edwardsville
   Box 1047
   Edwardsville 62026

St. Xavier University
   3700 West 103rd Street
   Chicago 60655

University of Illinois at Urbana-Champaign
   506 South Wright Street
   Urbana 61801

Western Illinois University
   900 West Adams Street
   Macomb 61455-1383

Indiana

Anderson University
   Anderson 46012

Ball State University
   2000 University Avenue
   Muncie 47306

Butler University
  Forty-Sixth and Sunset Avenue
  Indianapolis 46208

Franklin College
  Monroe Street
  Franklin 46131

Indiana State University
  217 North Sixth Street
  Terra Haute 47809

Indiana University-Bloomington
  814 East Third Street
  Bloomington 47405

Indiana University-Kokomo
  P.O. Box 9003
  Kokomo 46904-9003

Indiana University-Northwest
  3400 Broadway
  Gary 46408

Indiana University-South Bend
  P.O. Box 7111-1700 Mishawaka Avenue
  South Bend 46634

Indiana University-Southeast
  4201 Grant Line Road
  New Albany 47150

Marian College
  3200 Cold Spring Road
  Indianapolis 46222

Purdue University
  Schleman Hall
  West Lafayette 47907

Purdue University-Calumet
  2233 171st Street
  Hammond 46323

St. Francis College
  2701 Spring Street
  Fort Wayne 46808

St. Mary of the Woods College
  St. Mary of the Woods 47876

University of Evansville
    1800 East Lincoln Avenue
    Evansville 47722

University of Indianapolis
    1400 East Hanna Avenue
    Indianapolis 46227

Valparaiso University
    Valparaiso 46383

Iowa

Buena Vista College
    610 West Fourth Street
    Storm Lake 50588

Central College
    812 University Street
    Pella 50219

Clarke College
    1550 Clarke Drive
    Dubuque 52001

Iowa State University
    Alumni Hall
    Ames 50011

Loras College
    1450 Alta Vista
    Dubuque 52001

Morningside College
    1501 Morningside Aveune
    Sioux City 51106

Northwestern College
    101 College Avenue
    Orange City 51041

St. Ambrose College
    518 West Locust Street
    Davenport 52803

University of Dubuque
    2000 University Avenue
    Dubuque 52001

University of Northern Iowa
    West Twenty-Seventh Street
    Cedar Falls 50614

Wartburg College
P.O. Box 1003-222
Ninth Street NW
Waverly 50677

Kansas

Benedictine College
North Campus
Atchison 66002

Bethel College
300 East Twenty-Seventh Street
North Newton 67117

Emporia State University
Twelfth and Commercial Streets
Emporia 66801

Fort Hayes State University
600 Park Street
Hays 67601

Kansas Wesleyan University
100 East Clarifin
Salina 67401

McPherson College
1600 East Euclid
McPherson 67460

Pittsburg State University
1701 South Broadway
Pittsburg 66762

Saint Mary College
4100 South Fourth Street
Leavenworth 66048

Sterling College
North Broadway
Sterling 67579

Tabor College
Hillsboro 67073

Wichita State University
8545 Fairmount Street
Wichita 67208

Kentucky

Bellarmine College
2001 Newburg Road
Louisville 40205-0671

Brescia College
717 Frederica Street
Owensboro 42301

Cumberland College
6178 College Station Drive
Williamsburg 40769

Eastern Kentucky University
Lancaster Avenue
Richmond 40475

Morehead State University
Morehead 40351

Murray State University
Murray 42071

Northern Kentucky University
Nunn Drive
Highland Heights 41099-7010

Pikeville College
Sycamore Street
Pikesville 41501

University of Kentucky
100 Funkhouser Building
Lexington 40506

University of Louisville
Louisville 40292

Western Kentucky University
Wetherby Administration Building Room 209
Bowling Green 42101

Louisiana

Dillard University
2601 Gentilly Boulevard
New Orleans 70122-3097

Grambling State University
Grambling 71245

Louisiana College
P.O. Box 560
Pineville 71359

Louisiana State University
110 Thomas Boyd Hall
Baton Rouge 70803

Louisiana State University-Shreveport
One University Place
Shreveport 71115

Louisiana Tech University
P.O. Box 3168 Tech Station
Ruston 71272

McNeese State University
Lake Charles 70609

Nicholls State University
P.O. Box 2004 University Station
Thibodaux 70310

Northeast Louisiana University
700 University Avenue
Monroe 71209

Northwestern State University of Louisiana
College Avenue
Natchitoches 71497

Southeastern Louisiana University
Box 752-University Station
Hammond 70402

Southern University-Baton Rouge
P.O. Box 9901-Southern Branch
Baton Rouge 70813

University of Southwestern Louisiana
P.O. Box 41770
Lafayette 70504

Xavier University of Louisiana
7325 Palmetto Street
New Orleans 70125

Maine

University of Maine at Farmington
102 Main Street
Farmington 04938

Maryland

Bowie State University
Jericho Park Road
Bowie 20715

College of Notre Dame of Maryland
4701 North Charles Street
Baltimore 21210

Coppin State College
2500 West North Avenue
Baltimore 21216

Goucher College
1021 Dulaney Valley Road
Baltimore 21204

Hood College
Rosemont Avenue
Frederick 21701

Loyola College
4501 North Charles Street
Baltimore 21210

University of Maryland at College Park
College Park 20742

University of Maryland-Eastern Shore
Princess Anne 21853

Massachusetts

American International College
1000 State Street
Springfield 01109

Boston College
Lyons Hall-Room 120
Chestnut Hill 02167

Bridgewater State College
Bridgewater 02325

Curry College
1071 Blue Hill Road
Milton 02186

Fitchburg State College
160 Pearl Street
Fitchburg 01420

Gordon College
    255 Grapevine Road
    Wenham 01984

Lesley College
    29 Everett Street
    Cambridge 02138-2790

Simmons College
    300 The Fenway
    Boston 02115

Tufts University
    Medford 02155

Westfield State College
    Western Avenue
    Westfield 01086

Wheelock College
    200 The Riverway
    Boston 02215

Michigan

Andrews University
    Berrien Springs 49104

Aquinas College
    1607 Robinson Road SE
    Grand Rapids 49506-1799

Calvin College
    Grand Rapids 49506

Central Michigan University
    100 Warriner Hall
    Mount Pleasant 48859

Eastern Michigan University
    400 Pierce Hall
    Silanti 48197

Grand Valley State University
    1 Seidman House
    Allendale 49401-9401

Hope College
    Holland 49423

Madonna University
    36600 Schoolcraft Road
    Livonia 48150

Marygrove College
   8425 West McNichols Road
   Detroit 48221

Michigan State University
   Administration Building-Room 250
   East Lansing 48824

Northern Michigan University
   Cohodas Administration Center
   Marquette 49855

University of Detroit-Mercy
   4001 West McNichols Road
   Detroit 48221

University of Michigan-Ann Arbor
   515 East Jefferson-Room 1220
   Ann Arbor 48109

Wayne State University
   Detroit 48202

Western Michigan University
   Administration Building
   Kalamazoo 49008

Minnesota

Bemidji State University
   Bemidji 56601

Moorhead State University
   1104 Seventh Avenue South
   Moorhead 56560

St. Cloud State University
   Seventh Street and Fourth Avenue South
   St. Cloud 56301

University of Minnesota-Duluth
   184 Darland Administration Building
   Duluth 55801

University of Minnesota-Twin Cities
   Minneapolis 55455-0213

Winona State University
   Winona 55987

Mississippi

Alcorn State University
    P.O. Box 300
    Lorman 39096

Blue Mountain College
    Blue Mountain 38610

Delta State University
    P.O. Box 3151
    Cleveland 38732

Jackson State University
    1325 J. R. Lynch Street
    Jackson 39217

Mississippi College
    P.O. Box 4203
    Clinton 39058

Mississippi State University
    Box 5268
    Mississippi State 39762

Mississippi University for Women
    Columbus 39701

Tougaloo College
    Tougaloo 39174

University of Mississippi
    Lyceum Building
    University 38677

University of Southern Mississippi
    Box 5011-Southern Station
    Hattiesburg 39406

William Carey College
    Tuscan Avenue
    Hattiesburg 39401

Missouri

Avila College
    11901 Wornall Road
    Kansas City 64145

Central Missouri State University
    Warrensburg 64093

Culver Stockton College
    Canton 63435

Drury College
    900 North Benton Avenue
    Springfield 65802

Evangel College
    1111 North Glenstone
    Springfield 65802

Fontbonne College
    6800 Wydon Boulevard
    St. Louis 63105

Harris Stowe State College
    3026 Laclede Avenue
    St. Louis 63103

Lincoln University
    820 Chestnut Street
    Jefferson City 65101

Lindenwood College
    St. Charles 63301-4949

Missouri Southern State College
    Newman and Duquesne Roads
    Joplin 64801

Missouri Valley College
    500 East College
    Marshall 65340

Missouri Western State College
    4525 Downs Drive
    St. Joseph 64507

Northwest Missouri State University
    Maryville 64468

Southeast Missouri State University
    One University Plaza
    Cape Girardeau 63701

Southwest Missouri State University
    901 South National
    Springfield 65804

St. Louis University
    221 North Grand Boulevard
    St. Louis 63103

Stephens College
   Columbia 65215

University of Missouri-Columbia
   130 Jesse Hall
   Columbia 65211

University of Missouri-St. Louis
   8001 Natural Bridge Road
   St. Louis 63121

Webster University
   470 East Lockwood
   St. Louis 63119

Westminster College
   Seventh and Westminster Avenues
   Fulton 65251

William Woods College
   Fulton 65251

Montana

Carrol College
   North Benton Avenue
   Helena 59625

Eastern Montana College
   1500 North Thirtieth Street
   Billings 59101

Montana State University
   Montana Hall
   Bozeman 59717

Nebraska

Chadron State College
   Tenth and Main Streets
   Chadron 69337

College of Saint Mary
   1901 South Seventy-Second Street
   Omaha 68124

Concordia College
   800 North Columbia Avenue
   Seward 68434

Creighton University
  California at Twenty-Fourth Street
  Omaha 68178

Dana College
  2848 College Drive
  Blair 68008-1099

Doane College
  Crete 68333

Hastings College
  Seventh and Turner Avenues
  Hastings 68901

Nebraska Wesleyan University
  5000 St. Paul Avenue
  Lincoln 68504

Peru State College
  Peru 68421

University of Nebraska at Kearney
  905 West Twenty-Fifth Street
  Kearney 68849

University of Nebraska-Lincoln
  Fourteenth and R Streets
  Lincoln 68588-0415

University of Nebraska-Omaha
  Sixtieth and Dodge Streets
  Omaha 68182

Wayne State College
  200 East Tenth Street
  Wayne 68787

Nevada

University of Nevada-Las Vegas
  4505 Maryland Parkway
  Las Vegas 89154

University of Nevada-Reno
  Reno 89557

New Hampshire

Keene State College
  Main Street
  Keene 03431

Notre Dame College
   2321 Elm Street
   Manchester 03104

Rivier College
   South Main Street
   Nashua 03060

University of New Hampshire
   Garrison Avenue-Grant House
   Durham 03824

New Jersey

Centenary College
   400 Jefferson Street
   Hackettstown 07840

College of Saint Elizabeth
   Madison Avenue
   Convent Station 07961

Felician College
   260 South Main Street
   Lodi 07644

Georgian Court College
   900 Lakewood Avenue
   Lakewood 08701

Glassboro State College
   Glassboro 08028

Jersey City State College
   2039 Kennedy Boulevard
   Jersey City 07305

Kean College of New Jersey
   Morris Avenue
   Union 07083

Monmouth College
   Cedar Avenue
   West Long Branch 07764

Rutgers-The State University of New Jersey
   Douglass College
   P.O. Box 2101
   New Brunswick 08903

Rutgers-The State University of New Jersey
Livingston College
P.O. Box 2101
New Brunswick 08903

Rutgers-The State University of New Jersey
Rutgers College
P.O. Box 2101
New Brunswick 08903

Seton Hall University
400 South Orange Avenue
South Orange 07079

Trenton State College
Hillwood Lakes CN 4700
Trenton 08650-4700

William Patterson College
300 Pompton Road
Wayne 07470

New Mexico

College of the Southwest
6610 Lovington Highway
Hobbs 88240

Eastern New Mexico University
Station Seven
Portales 88130

New Mexico State University
Box 30001-Department 3A
Las Cruces 88003-0001

University of New Mexico
Albuquerque 87131

Western New Mexico University
P.O. Box 680
Silver City 88061

New York

Adelphi University
South Avenue
Garden City 11530

College of Mount Saint Vincent
   263rd Street and Riverdale Avenue
   New York 10471

College of New Rochelle
   College of Arts and Sciences and School of Nursing
   Castle Place
   New Rochelle 10805

College of Saint Rose
   432 Western Avenue
   Albany 12203

CUNY-Baruch College
   17 Lexington Avenue
   New York 10010

CUNY-Brooklyn College
   Bedford Avenue and Avenue H
   Brooklyn 11210

CUNY-City College
   Convent Avenue at 138th Street
   New York 10031

CUNY-College of Staten Island
   715 Ocean Terrace
   Staten Island 10301

CUNY-Lehman College
   Bedford Park Boulevard West
   Bronx 10468

CUNY-Medgar Evers College
   1615 Bedford Avenue
   Brooklyn 11225-2201

CUNY-York College
   94-20 Guy R. Brewer Boulevard
   Jamaica 11451

D'Yourville College
   320 Porter Avenue
   Buffalo 14201

Daemen College
   4380 Main Street
   Amhurst 14226

Dominican College of Blauvelt
10 Western Highway
Orangeburg 10962

Dowling College
Idle Hour Boulevard
Oakdale 11769

Hobart and William Smith Colleges
Geneva 14456

Iona College
715 North Avenue
New Rochelle 10801

Keuka College
Keuka Park 14478

LeMoyne College
Syracuse 13214-1399

Long Island University-C. W. Post Campus
Northern Boulevard-College Hall
Greenvale 11548

Manhattan College
Manhattan College Parkway
Riverdale 10471

Marist College
North Road
Poughkeepsie 12601

Marymount College
Tarrytown 10591

Marymount Manhattan College
221 East Seventy-First Street
New York 10021

Mercy College
555 Broadway
Dobbs Ferry 10522

Molloy College
1000 Hempstead Avenue
Rockville Center 11570

Mount Saint Mary College
330 Powell Avenue
Newburgh 12550

Nazareth College of Rochester
4245 East Avenue
Rochester 14610

New York University
22 Washington Square North
New York 10011

Russel Sage College
51 First Street
Troy 12180

Saint John's University
Grand Central and Utopia Parkways
Jamaica 11439

Saint Joseph's College
245 Clinton Avenue
Brooklyn 11205

Saint Joseph's College-Suffolk
155 Roe Boulevard
Patchogue 11772

Saint Thomas Aquinas College
Route 340
Sparkill 10968

SUNY-College at Buffalo
1300 Elmwood Avenue
Buffalo 14222

SUNY-College at Fredonia
Fredonia 14063

SUNY-College at Geneseo
Erwin Administration Building
Geneseo 14454-1471

SUNY-College at New Paltz
75 South Manheim Boulevard
New Paltz 12561-2499

SUNY-College at Old Westbury
P.O. Box 307
Old Westbury 11568

SUNY-College at Plattsburgh
Plattsburgh 12901

Syracuse University
    200 Administration Building
    Syracuse 13244

Vassar College
    Raymond Avenue
    Poughkeepsie 12601

Wagner College
    631 Howard Avenue
    Staten Island 10301

North Carolina

Appalachian State University
    Boone 29608

Belmont Abbey College
    Belmont 28012

Bennett College
    900 East Washington Street
    Greensboro 27401

Catawba College
    2300 West Innes Street
    Salisbury 28144

East Carolina University
    Greenville 27834

Elizabeth City State University
    Parkview Drive
    Elizabeth City 27909

Greensboro College
    815 West Market Street
    Greensboro 27410

High Point University
    University Station-Montlieu Avenue
    High Point 27262-3598

Lenoir-Rhyne College
    Box 7227
    Hickory 28603

Livingstone College
    701 West Monroe Street
    Salisbury 28114

Methodist College
    5400 Ramsay Street
    Fayetteville 28311-1499

Pembroke State University
    Pembroke 28372

Salem College
    P.O. Box 10548
    Winston-Salem 27108

Shaw University
    118 East South Street
    Raleigh 27611

St. Augustine's College
    1315 Oak Avenue
    Raleigh 27610-2298

University of North Carolina-Asheville
    One University Heights
    Asheville 28804

University of North Carolina-Charlotte
    University City Boulevard
    Charlotte 28223

University of North Carolina-Wilmington
    601 South College Road
    Wilmington 28403

Western Carolina University
    520 H. F. Robinson Administration Building
    Cullowhee 28723

Winston-Salem State University
    601 Martin Luther King, Jr., Drive
    Winston-Salem 27110

North Dakota

Dickinson State Univesity
    Dickinson 58601

Minot State University
    Minot 58707

University of Mary
    7500 University Drive
    Bismarck 58504

University of North Dakota
  Grand Forks 58202

Ohio

Ashland University
  College Avenue
  Ashland 44805

Baldwin-Wallace College
  275 Eastland Road
  Berea 44017

Bluffton College
  Box 638-Marbeck Center
  Bluffton 45817

Bowling Green State University
  110 McFall Center
  Bowling Green 43403

Cedarville College
  Box 601
  Cedarville 45314

Central State University
  Brush Row Road
  Wilberforce 45384

Cleveland State University
  East Twenty-Fourth and Euclid Avenue
  Cleveland 44115

College of Mount Saint Joseph
  5701 Delhi Road
  Cincinnati 45233-9314

The Defiance College
  701 North Clinton Street
  Defiance 43512

Franciscan University of Steubenville
  Franciscan Way
  Steubenville 43952

Heidelberg College
  310 East Market Street
  Tiffin 44883

Hiram College
  P.O. Box 96
  Hiram 44234

Kent State University
  P.O. Box 5190
  Kent 44242-0001

Malone College
  515 Twenty-Fifth Street NW
  Canton 44708

Miami University
  Oxford 45056

Mount Union College
  1972 Clark Avenue
  Alliance 44601

Mount Vernon Nazarene College
  800 Martinsburg Road
  Mount Vernon 43050

Muskingum College
  New Concord 43762

Notre Dame College of Ohio
  4545 College Road
  Cleveland 44121

Ohio Dominican College
  1216 Sunbury Road
  Columbus 43219

Ohio Northern University
  Main Street
  Ada 45810

Ohio State University-Columbus
  1800 Cannon Drive-1210 Lincoln Tower
  Columbus 43210

Ohio University
  120 Chubb Hall
  Athens 45701

University of Akron
  381 E. Buchtel Commons
  Akron 44325-2001

University of Cincinnati
  100 French Hall
  Cincinnati 45221

University of Dayton
   300 College Park
   Dayton 45469

University of Findlay
   1000 North Main Street
   Findlay 45840

University of Rio Grande
   P.O. Box 909
   Rio Grande 45674

University of Toledo
   2801 West Bancroft Street
   Toledo 43606

Urbana University
   579 College Way
   Urbana 43078-2091

Ursuline College
   2550 Lander Road
   Pepper Pike 44124

Walsh College
   2020 Easton Street NW
   North Canton 44720

Wittenburg University
   P.O. Box 720
   Springfield 45501

Wright State University
   Colonel Glenn Highway
   Dayton 45435

Xavier University
   3800 Victory Parkway
   Cincinnati 45207

Youngstown State University
   Youngstown 44555

Oklahoma

Cameron University
   2800 Gore Boulevard
   Lawton 73505

East Central University
   Ada 74820-6899

Northeastern State University
    Tahlequah 74464

Northwestern State University
    709 Oklahoma Boulevard
    Alva 73717

Oklahoma State University
    103 Whitehurst Hall
    Stillwater 74078

Southwestern Oklahoma State University
    Weatherford 73096

University of Central Oklahoma
    Edmond 73034-0172

University of Oklahoma-Norman
    1000 Asp Avenue
    Norman 73019

University of Science and Arts of Oklahoma
    Seventeenth Street and Grand Avenue
    Chickasha 73018

Oregon

University of Oregon
    240 Oregon Hall
    Eugene 97403

University of Portland
    5000 North Willamette Boulevard
    Portland 97203

Warner Pacific College
    2219 Southeast Sixty-Eighth Street
    Portland 97215

Western Oregon State College
    Monmouth 97361

Pennsylvania

Beaver College
    Church and Easton Roads
    Glenside 19038

Bloomsburg University of Pennsylvania
    Ben Franklin Building

Bloomsburg 17815

Cabrini College
610 King of Prussia Road
Radnor 19087-3699

California University of Pennsylvania
250 University Avenue
California 15419-1394

Carlow College
3333 Fifth Avenue
Pittsburgh 15213

Cheyney University of Pennsylvania
Cheney 19319

Clarion University of Pennsylvania
Clarion 16214

College Misericordia
Lake Street
Dalla 18612

Duquesne University
600 Forbes Avenue
Pittsburgh 15282

East Stroudsburg University of Pennsylvania
East Stroudsburg 18301

Edinboro University of Pennsylvania
Edinboro 16444

Gannon University
University Square
Erie 16541

Gannon University-Villa Marie Campus
2551 West Lake Road
Erie 16505

Gwynedd-Mercy College
Sumneytown Pike
Gwynedd Valley 19437

Holy Family College
Grant and Frankford Avenues
Philadelphia 19114

Indiana University of Pennsylvania
Indiana 15705

King's College
  133 North River Street
  Wilkes-Barre 18711

Kutztown University
  College Hill
  Kutztown 19530

LaSalle University
  Olney Avenue at Twentieth Street
  Philadelphia 19141

Lincoln University
  Lincoln Hall
  Lincoln University 19352

Lock Haven University of Pennsylvania
  Lock Haven 17745

Mansfield University of Pennsylvania
  Alumni Hall
  Mansfield 16933

Marywood College
  2300 Adams Avenue
  Scranton 18509

Mercyhurst College
  Glenwood Hills
  Erie 16546

Millersville University of Pennsylvania
  P.O. Box 1002
  Millersville 17551-0302

Penn State-University Park
  201 Shields Building
  University Park 16802

Slippery Rock University of Pennsylvania
  Slippery Rock 16057

Temple University
  Philadelphia 19122

Villanova University
  Villanova 19085

West Chester University of Pennsylvania
  West Chester 19383

Puerto Rico

American University of Puerto Rico
P.O. Box 2037
Bayamon 00621

Inter-American University of Puerto Rico
Arecibo Campus
Call Box UI
Arecibo 00613

Pontifical Catholic University of Puerto Rico
Las Americas Avenue-Station Six
Ponce 00731

University of Puerto Rico
Rio Piedras Campus
P.O. Box 22334 UPR Station
Rio Piedras 00931

Rhode Island

Providence College
River Avenue
Providence 02918

Rhode Island College
Providence 02908

Salve Regina University
Ochre Point Avenue
Newport 02840-4192

South Carolina

Central Wesleyan College
Central 29630

Coker College
College Avenue
Hartsville 29550

College of Charleston
Sixty-Six George Street
Charleston 29424

Columbia College
1301 Columbia College Drive
Columbia 29203

Converse College
    580 East Main Street
    Spartanburg 29301

Erskine College
    Due West 29639

Furman University
    3200 Poinsett Highway
    Greenville 29613-0645

Lander University
    Stanley Avenue
    Greenwood 29649

Presbyterian College
    Broad Street
    Clinton 29325

South Carolina State University
    Orangeburg 29117-0001

Winthrop University
    Oakland Avenue
    Rock Hill 29733

South Dakota

Augustana College
    Twenty-Ninth and Summit Avenue
    Sioux Falls 57197

Black Hills State University
    1200 University Street
    Spearfish 57783

Dakota State University
    Heston Hall
    Madison 57042

Northern State University
    Aberdeen 57401

Sioux Falls College
    1501 South Prairie Street
    Sioux Falls 57105

University of South Dakota
    414 East Clark
    Vermillion 57069

Tennessee

Austin Peay State University
P.O. Box 4548
Clarksville 37040

Belmont University
1900 Belmont Boulevard
Nashville 37212

Bryan College
Box 7000
Dayton 37321

Carson-Newman College
Russell Avenue
Jefferson City 37760

East Tennessee State University
Campus Box 244030-A
Johnson City 37614

Freed-Hardeman University
158 East Main Street
Henderson 38340

Lambuth College
Lambuth Boulevard
Jackson 38301

Memphis State University
Memphis 38152

Middle Tennessee State University
Murfreesboro 37132

Tennessee State University
3500 John Merritt Boulevard
Nashville 37203

Tennessee Technological University
Dixie Avenue
Cookeville 38505

Union University
2447 Highway 45 By-Pass
Jackson 38305

University of Tennessee-Chattanooga
McCallie Avenue-129 Hooper Hall
Chattanooga 37403

University of Tennessee-Knoxville
320 Student Services Building
Knoxville 37996-0230

University of Tennessee-Martin
Martin 38238

Vanderbilt University
2305 West End Avenue
Nashville 37203

Texas

Angelo State University
2601 West Avenue N
San Angelo 76909

Baylor University
P.O. Box 97008
Waco 76798-7008

Corpus Christi State University
6300 Ocean Drive
Corpus Christi 78412

East Texas State University
East Texas Station
Commerce 75429

Incarnate Word College
4301 Broadway
San Antonio 78209

Lamar University
P.O. Box 10009
Beaumont 77710

Laredo State University
One West End Washington Street
Laredo 78040-0960

Midwestern State University
3400 Taft Boulevard
Wichita Falls 76308

Our Lady of the Lake-University of San Antonio
411 Southwest Twenty-Fourth Street
San Antonio 78207-4689

Prairie View A and M University
P.O. Box 2610
Prairie View 77446

Sam Huston State University
   Huntsville 77341

Southwest Texas State University
   J. C. Kellam Building
   San Marcos 78666

Stephen F. Austin State University
   Nacogdoches 75962

Texas Southern University
   3100 Cleburne
   Houston 77004

Texas Technical University
   P.O. Box 42017
   Lubbock 79409

Texas Women's University
   P.O. Box 22909-TWU Station
   Denton 76204

University of Houston-Clear Lake
   2700 Bay Area Boulevard
   Houston 77058

University of Mary Hardin-Baylor
   P.O. Box 403
   Belton 76513

University of Saint Thomas
   3812 Montrose
   Houston 77006

University of Texas-Austin
   Austin 78712

University of Texas-El Paso
   El Paso 79968

University of Texas-Permian Basin
   Box 8422-UTPB
   Odessa 79762

University of Texas-Tyler
   3900 University Boulevard
   Tyler 75701

West Texas State University
   Canyon 79016

Utah

University of Utah
   250 Student Services Building
   Salt Lake City 84112

Utah State University
   Logan 84322

Vermont

Castleton State College
   Castleton 05735

College of Saint Joseph in Vermont
   Clement Road-St. Joseph Hall
   Rutland 05701

Green Mountain College
   16 College Street
   Poultney 05764

Johnson State College
   Stowe Road
   Johnson 05656

Lyndon State College
   Lyndonville 05851

Trinity College
   208 Colechester Avenue
   Burlington 05401

University of Vermont
   194 South Prospect Street
   Burlington 05401-3596

Virginia

Eastern Mennonite College
   Harrisburg 22801

Hampton University
   Hampton 23668

James Madison University
   Harrisonburg 22807

Longwood College
   Farmville 23909

Lynchburg College
  1501 Lakeside Drive
  Lynchburg 24501

Mary Baldwin College
  Staunton 24401

Norfolk State University
  2401 Corprew Avenue
  Norfolk 23529-0050

Old Dominion University
  Hampton Boulevard
  Norfolk 23529-0050

Radford University
  Radford 24142

Virginia Commonwealth University
  P.O. Box 2526-821 West Franklin Street
  Richmond 23284-2526

Virginia State University
  Box 9018
  Petersburg 23806

Virginia Union University
  1500 North Lombardy Street
  Richmond 23220

Washington

Central Washington University
  Mitchell Hall
  Ellensburg 98926

Eastern Washington University
  Showalter Hall-Room 117
  Cheney 99004

Gonzaga University
  Spokane 99258

Saint Martin's College
  5300 Pacific Avenue SE
  Lacey 98503-1297

Seattle Pacific University
  3307 Third Avenue West
  Seattle 98119

Washington State University
342 French Administration Building
Pullman 99164

Western Washington University
Old Main-Room 200
Bellingham 98225

Whitworth College
Spokane 99251

West Virginia

Alderson-Broadus College
Phillippi 26416

Bethany College
Bethany 26032

Bluefield State College
Bluefield 24701

Concord College
Athens 24712

Fairmont State College
Locust Avenue Extension
Fairmont 26554

Glenville State College
Glenville 26351

Marshall University
400 Hal Greer Boulevard
Huntington 25755

West Liberty State College
West Liberty 26074

West Virginia University
P.O. Box 6009
Morgantown 26506-6009

Wisconsin

Cardinal Stritch College
6801 North Yates Road
Milwaukee 53217

Carthage College
2001 Alford Park Drive
Kenosha 53140-1994

Edgewood College
  855 Woodrow Street
  Madison 53711

Siler Lake College
  2406 South Alverno Road
  Manitowoc 54220

University of Wisconsin-Eau Claire
  Eau Claire 54701

University of Wisconsin-Milwaukee
  P.O. Box 749
  Milwaukee 53201

University of Wisconsin-Oshkosh
  135 Dempsey Hall
  Oshkosh 54901

University of Wisconsin-Stevens Point
  Stevens Point 54481

University of Wisconsin-Whitewater
  800 West Main Street
  Whitewater 53190

Wyoming

University of Wyoming
  Box 3435-University Station
  Laramie 82071

CANADIAN UNIVERSITIES

Alberta

University of Alberta
  Edmondton, Alberta T6G 2E8

University of Calgary
  2500 University Drive NW
  Calgary, Alberta T2N 1N4

University of Lethbridge
  4401 University Drive
  Lethbridge, Alberta T1K 3M4

British Columbia

University of British Columbia
  Vancouver, British Columbia V6T 1Z2

University of Victoria
   P.O. Box 1700
   Victoria, British Columbia U8W 2Y2

Manitoba

University of Manitoba
   Winnipeg, Manitoba R3T 2N2

New Brunswick

University of New Brunswick
   Fredrickton, New Brunswick E3B 5A3

Nova Scotia

University College of Cape Breton
   P.O. Box 5300
   Sidney, Nova Scotia B1P 6L2

University of Kings College
   Halifax, Nova Scotia B3H 2A1

Ontario

University of Ottawa
   Ottawa, Ontario K1N 6N5

University of Toronto
   Toronto, Ontario M5S 1A1

University of Waterloo
   Waterloo, Ontario N2L 3G1

University of Western Ontario
   London, Ontario N6B 3P4

University of Windsor
   Windsor, Ontario N9B 3P4

Prince Edward Island

University of Prince Edward Island
   550 University Avenue
   Charlottetown, Prince Edward Island C1A 4B3

Saskatchewan

University of Regina
   Regina, Saskatchewan S4S 0A2

University of Saskatchewan
   Saskatoon, Saskatchewan S7N 0W8

SCHOOLS FOR INDUSTRIAL ENGINEERING TECHNICIANS

Alabama

Alabama A and M University
  P.O. Box 284
  Normal 35762

Arizona

Arizona State University
  Tempe 85287-0112

DeVry Institute of Technology
  2149 West Dunlap Avenue
  Phoenix 85021-2995

Arkansas

Arkansas State University
  P.O. Box 1630
  State University 72467

University of Arkansas-Pine Bluff
  1200 University Drive
  Pine Bluff 71601-2799

California

California Polytechnic State University
  San Luis Obispo 93407

California State Polytechnic University-Pomona
3801 West Temple Avenue
Pomona 91768

California State University-Chico
Chico 95929-0850

California State University-Fresno
Shaw and Cedar Avenues
Fresno 93740

California State University-Long Beach
1250 Bellflower Boulevard
Long Beach 90840

California State University-Los Angeles
5151 State University Drive
Los Angeles 90032

California State University-San Bernardino
5500 University Parkway
San Bernardino 92407-2397

Coleman College
7380 Parkway Drive
La Mesa 92041

National University
University Park
San Diego 92108-4194

San Jose State University
One Washington Square
San Jose 95192-0009

West Coast University
440 Shatto Place
Los Angeles 90020-1765

Colorado

Adams State University
Alamosa 81102

Colorado State University
Administration Annex
Fort Collins 80523

Colorado Technical University
4435 North Chestnut Drive
Colorado Springs 80907

University of Southern Colorado
  2200 Bonforte Avenue
  Pueblo 81001

Connecticut

Central Connecticut State University
  1615 Stanley Street
  New Britain 06050

University of New Haven
  300 Orange Avenue
  West Haven 06516

Delaware

Delaware State University
  1200 North DuPont Highway
  Dover 19901

Florida

Florida Agricultural and Mechanical University
  Tallahassee 32307

University of Central Florida
  P.O. Box 160111
  Orlando 32816-0111

University of North Florida
  4567 St. John Bluff Road, South
  Jacksonville 32224

University of West Florida
  11000 University Parkway
  Pensacola 32514

Georgia

Berry College
  P.O. Box 159-Mount Berry Station
  Mount Berry 30149

Georgia Southern University
  Box 024
  Statesboro 30458

Savannah State College
  State College Branch
  Savannah 31404

Southern College of Technology
   1100 South Marietta Parkway
   Marietta 30060-2896

Idaho

Idaho State University
   P.O. Box 8054
   Pocatello 83209

University of Idaho
   141 Administration Building
   Moscow 83844-3133

Illinois

Bradley University
   1501 West Bradley
   Peoria 61625

DeVry Institute of Technology
   3300 North Campbell Avenue
   Chicago 60618-5994

Eastern Illinois University
   Old Main-Room 116
   Charleston 61920

Illinois State University
   Campus Box 2200
   Normal 61761

Northern Illinois University
   DeKalb 60115

Roosevelt University
   430 South Michigan Avenue
   Chicago 60605

Southern Illinois University at Carbondale
   Woody Hall
   Carbondale 62901

Western Illinois University
   900 West Adams Street
   Macomb 61455-1383

Indiana

Ball State University
  2000 University Avenue
  Muncie 47306

University of Southern Indiana
  8600 University Boulevard
  Evansville 47712

Indiana State University
  Tirey Hall
  Terre Haute 47809

Indiana University-Purdue University at Fort Wayne
  2101 Coliseum Boulevard East
  Fort Wayne 46805

Indiania University-Purdue University at Indianapolis
  425 University Boulevard/Cavanaugh Hall Room 129
  Indianapolis 46202-5143

Purdue University
  Schleman Hall
  West Lafayette 47907

Purdue University-North Central
  1401 South U.S. Highway 421
  Westville 46391

Iowa

University of Northern Iowa
  West Twenty-Seventh Street
  Cedar Falls 50614

William Penn College
  201 Trueblood Avenue
  Oskaloosa 52577

Kansas

Kansas State University
  Anderson Hall
  Manhattan 66506

Pittsburg State University
  1701 South Broadway
  Pittsburg 66762

Kentucky

Eastern Kentucky University
  Lancaster Avenue
  Richmond 40475

Western Kentucky University
  Potter Hall
  1 Big Red Way
  Bowling Green 42101

Louisiana

Louisiana Tech University
  P.O. Box 3168-Tech Station
  Ruston 71272

McNeese State University
  Lake Charles 70609

Nicholls State University
  P.O. Box 2004-University Station
  Thibodaux 70310

Southern University-Baton Rouge
  P.O. Box 9901-Southern Branch
  Baton Rouge 70813

University of Southwestern Louisiana
  P.O. Box 41770
  Lafayette 70504

Maine

Maine Maritime Academy-The Ocean College
  Castine 04420

The University of Maine at Orono
  Chadbourne Hall
  Orono 04469

The University of Southern Maine
  37 College Avenue
  Gorham 04038

Maryland

Capitol College
  11301 Springfield Road
  Laurel 20708

University of Maryland at College Park
    College Park 20742

Massachusetts

Fitchburg State College
    160 Pearl Street
    Fitchburg 01420

Northeastern University
    360 Huntington Avenue
    Boston 02115

University of Massachusetts-Lowell
    One University Avenue
    Lowell 01854

Michigan

Andrews University
    Berrien Springs 49104

Central Michigan University
    100 Warriner Hall
    Mount Pleasant 48859

Eastern Michigan University
    400 Pierce Hall
    Ypsilanti 48197

Ferris State University
    Big Rapids 49307

Lawrence Technological University
    21000 West Ten Mile Road
    Southfield 48075

Northern Michigan University
    Cohodes Administration Center
    Marquette 49855

Saginaw Valley State University
    2250 Pierce Road
    University Center 48710

Wayne State University
    Detroit 48202

Western Michigan University
    Administration Building
    Kalamazoo 49008

Minnesota

Moorhead State University
1104 Seventy-Fourth Avenue South
Moorhead 56560

St. Cloud State University
Seventh Street and Fourth Avenue South
St. Cloud 56301

Mississippi

Alcorn State University
P.O. Box 300
Lorman 39096

Jackson State University
1325 J. R. Lynch Street
Jackson 39217

Mississippi Valley State University
14000 Highway 82 West
Itta Bena 38941

University of Southern Mississippi
Box 5011-Southern Station
Hattiesburg 39406

Missouri

Central Missouri State University
Warrensburg 64093

DeVry Institute of Technology
11224 Holmes Road
Kansas City 64131-3626

Missouri Western State College
4525 Downs Drive
St. Joseph 64507

Southwest Missouri State University
901 South National
Springfield 65804

University of Missouri-Rolla
102 Parker Hall
Rolla 65401

Washington University
Campus Box 1089
St. Louis 63130

Montana

Northern Montana College
    Havre 59501

Nebraska

   Chadron State College
   Tenth and Main Streets
   Chadron 69337

Peru State College
    Peru 68421

University of Nebraska-Omaha
    Sixtieth and Dodge Streets
    Omaha 68182

New Hampshire

University of New Hampshire
    Garrison Avenue-Grant House
    Durham 03824

New Jersey

Fairleigh Dickenson University
    1000 River Road
    Teaneck 07666

Fairleigh Dickenson University-Rutherford
    270 Montross Avenue
    Rutherford 07070

Rowan College of New Jersey
    201 Mullica Hill Road
    Glassboro 08028-1701

Kean College of New Jersey
    1000 Morris Avenue
    Union 07083

New Jersey Institute of Technology
    Newark 07102-9938

Trenton State College
    Hillwood Lakes CN 4700
    Trenton 08650-4700

New Mexico

New Mexico State University-Main Campus
Box 30001, Department 3A
Las Cruces 88003-0001

New York

Rochester Institute of Technology
P.O. Box 9887, One Lomb Memorial Drive
Rochester 14623

SUNY College at Buffalo
1300 Elmwood Avenue
Buffalo 14222

SUNY Institute of Technology at Utica, Rome
P.O. Box 3050
Utica 13504-3050

University of the State of New York
Regents College
7 Columbia Circle
Albany 12203-5159

North Carolina

East Carolina University
Greenville 27858

Elizabeth City State University
Parkview Drive
Elizabeth City 27909

North Carolina Agricultural and Technical State University
1601 East Market Street
Greensboro 27411

University of North Carolina-Charlotte
University City Boulevard
Charlotte 28223

Western Carolina University
520 H. F. Robinson Administration Building
Cullowhee 28723

North Dakota

North Dakota State University
124 Ceres Hall
Fargo 58102

University of North Dakota
    Grand Forks 58202

Ohio

Bowling Green State University
    110 McFall Center
    Bowling Green 43403

Cleveland State University
    East Twenty-Fourth and Euclid Avenue
    Cleveland 44115

DeVry Institute of Technology
    1350 Alum Creek Drive
    Columbus 43209-2764

Franklin University
    201 South Grant Avenue
    Columbus 43215-5399

Kent State University
    P.O. Box 5190
    Kent 44242-0001

Miami University
    Oxford 45056

Ohio Northern University
    525 South Main Street
    Ada 45810

University of Akron
    381 East Buchtel Commons
    Akron 44325-2001

University of Cincinnati
    100 Edwards Center-P.O. Box 210091
    Cincinnati 45221-0091

University of Dayton
    300 College Park
    Dayton 45469-1611

University of Toledo
    2801 West Bancroft Street
    Toledo 43606

Youngstown State University
    Youngstown 44555

Oklahoma

East Central University
  Ada 74820-6899

Langston University
  P.O. Box 838
  Langston 73050

Northeastern State University
  Tahlequah 74464

Oklahoma State University
  103 Whitehurst Hall
  Stillwater 74078

Southeastern Oklahoma State University
  Box 4118-Station A
  Durant 74701

Southwestern Oklahoma State University
  Weatherford 73096

Oregon

Oregon Institute of Technology
  3201 Campus Drive
  Klamath Falls 97601

Pennsylvania

California University of Pennsylvania
  250 University Avenue
  California 15419-1394

Cheyney University of Pennsylvania
  Cheyney 19319

Gannon University
  University Square
  Erie 16541

Millersville University of Pennsylvania
  P.O. Box 1002
  Millersville 17551-0302

Penn State-Erie
  The Behrend College
  Station Road
  Erie 16563

Penn State-Harrisburg
    The Capital College
    Middletown 17057

Penn State University Park
    201 Sheilds Building
    University Park 16802

Point Park College
    201 Wood Street
    Pittsburg 15222

Temple University
    Philadelphia 19122

University of Pennsylvania
    1 College Hall
    Philadelphia 19104

University of Pittsburg-Johnstown
    Johnstown 15904

South Carolina

South Carolina State University
    Orangeburg 29117-0001

South Dakota

Northern State University
    Aberdeen 57401

Tennessee

Austin Peay State University
    601 College Street
    Clarksville 37044

East Tennessee State University
    Campus Box 24430 A
    Johnson City 37614

Memphis State University
    Memphis 38152

Tennessee Technological University
    Dixie Avenue
    Cookeville 38505

Texas

Abilene Christian University
Box 6000-ACU Station
Abilene 79699

DeVry Institute of Technology
4250 North Beltline Road
Irving 75038-4299

East Texas State University
East Texas Station
Commerce 75429

Lamar University
P.O. Box 10009
Beaumont 77710

LeTourneau University
P.O. Box 7001
Longview 76507

Midwestern State University
3410 Taft Boulevard
Wichita Falls 76308

Sam Houston State University
Huntsville 77203

Southwest Texas State University
429 North Guadalupe
San Marcos 78666-5709

Sul Ross State University
P.O. Box C-1
Alpine 79832

Tarleton State University
Stephensville 76402

Texas A and M University
Office of Admissions and Records
217 John J. Koldus Building
College Station 77843-1265

Texas A and M University-Kingsville
Campus Box 116
Kingsville 78363

Texas Southern University
3100 Cleburne
Houston 77004

Texas Technical University
  P.O. Box 45005
  Lubbock 79409-5005

University of Houston
  4800 Calhoun
  Houston 77294-2161

University of Houston-Downtown
  One Main Street
  Houston 77002

University of North Texas
  Box 13797
  Denton 76203

West Texas State University
  Canyon 79016

Utah

Brigham Young University
  A-153 ASB
  Provo 84602

Weber State University
  3750 Harrison Boulevard
  Ogden 84408

Virginia

Old Dominion University
  Hampton Boulevard
  Norfolk 23529-0050

Virginia State University
  Box 9018
  Petersburg 23806

Washington

Central Washington University
  Mitchell Hall
  Ellensburg 98926

Eastern Washington University
  Showalter Hall-Room 117
  Cheney 99004

Walla Walla College
  College Place 99324

Western Washington University
    Old Main-Room 200
    Bellingham 98225

West Virginia

Bluefield State College
    Bluefield 24701

Fairmont State College
    Locust Avenue Extension
    Fairmont 26426

Salem Teikyo University
    Randolph Campus Center
    Salem 26426

West Virginia Institute of Technology
    Montgomery 25136

West Virginia State College
    Institute 25112

Wheeling Jesuit College
    316 Washington Avenue
    Wheeling 26003

Wisconsin

Milwaukee School of Engineering
    1025 North Broadway
    Milwaukee 53202-3109

University of Wisconsin-Parkside
    900 Wood Road
    Kenosha 53141-2000

University of Wisconsin-Stout
    130 Bowan Hall
    Menomonie 54751

SAMPLE RESUMES

Andrew Johnson
2716 North Hickory Avenue
Arlington Heights, Illinois 60004
(847) 555-2036

Job Title: Technical Writer

Writing Experience:

I wrote a weekly newspaper column for *The Northern Star* while I was an undergraduate student at Northern Illinois University. I write a column reviewing computer software offerings for Paddock Press. I also wrote the script for a video that trains teachers how to use a new video system in High School District 214.

Training Experience:

Writing Instructor at Harper College in Palatine, Illinois, from 1990 to 1995.

English Instructor at Fremd High School in Palatine, Illinois, from 1988 to 1990.

Software Experience:

Word processing and desktop publishing experience as a media specialist for the District Production Services at High School District 214 from 1986 to 1988.

Education:

Master of Arts in English, Northern Illinois University, 1986

Bachelor of Science in Business Education, Northern Illinois University, 1984.

References available upon request.

Angela Torres
2113 West Algonquin Parkway
Rolling Meadows, Illinois 60008
(847) 555-5787

Overview

I have four years experience with increasing responsibilities as a technical illustrator, with in-depth exposure to AutoCad engineering graphics, design, and drafting. I have experience in blueprint reading, dimensioning, tolerancing, assembly drawing, and airbrush illustration. I am seeking a position as a computer-aided designer in industrial design.

Skills

Over the past four years I have mastered the following skills:

—Detailed drawings of complex concepts in engineering graphics

—Assembly drawings and cutaways

—Airbrushing

—Computer applications on Cadd 4X computers

—Technical illustration in Freehand and Illustrator software

—Computer tracing from originals

—Desktop publishing with PageMaker and Ventura Publisher software, specializing in color applications

Accomplishments

Over the past four years I have:

—Developed detailed drawings of computer hardware

—Designed drafting blueprints of hardware using AutoCad software

—Illustrated brochures with Adobe software on the Macintosh

Employment

June 1995 to Present

Technical graphic artist at Johnson Engineering Company, Palatine, Illinois.

Education

Associate Degree in Applied Science
Harper College
Palatine, Illinois

References available upon request.

Oscar Arana
128 North Ridge Avenue
Naperville, Illinois 60162
(847) 555-2117

Objective:

I am seeking a position as a desktop publisher designing text and graphics in the field of electronic publishing.

Skills:

I have six years of experience as a desktop publisher using IBM and Macintosh computers. During this time I developed the skills to use the following hardware and software:

—IBM and compatible computers

—Macintosh computers

—Color or black-and-white scanners

—Color laser or inkjet printers

—Imagesetter, Linotronic, and Selectset

—CoreDraw, Ventura Publisher, Ventura AdPro, WordPerfect

—PageMaker, Toolbook for Windows, PhotoShop, and WordPerfect Presentations

Experience:

1991 to Present: Desktop publisher at Scott Foresman Company, Glenview, Illinois.

Education:

Associate Degree, Oakton College, Des Plaines, Illinois

Sabrina Owens
2901 West Central Road
Rolling Meadows, Illinois 60008
(847) 555-5601

Objective:

CADD project manager and senior drafter with four years experience seeks immediate opening using knowledge of computer-aided drafting.

Skills:

During the past four years I have acquired the following skills:

- AutoCad software experience and graphic design skills as an AutoCad drafter
- Used Intergraph, PC, Pencil, Ink, Leroy pins and templates
- Experience in drafting construction, drainage, street improvement, and site development plans
- Planned and supervised production of blueprints in a timely manner
- Developed and administered department budget

Education:

Associate Degree in Computer Science/Technology
Oakton College, Des Plaines, Illinois, 1995

References available on request.

James Chin
1241 West Thacker
Des Plaines, Illinois 60018
(847) 555-5787

Objective:

Human resources manager seeks a personnel management position in electronic publishing.

Experience:

I have three years experience in human resources in a high-pressure, high-technology environment, with two years experience in a supervisory position. My previous personal computer experience includes desktop publishing. I also have experience as an adult education instructor at the college level.

Achievements:

I managed the human resources department of a small company, and my job included the following responsibilities:

- Recruiting staff
- Administering salary and benefits for a staff of seventy-five people
- Creating and implementing training and development programs
- Creating and implementing wellness and safety programs for the staff

Employment:

1993 to Present: Human Resources Director
Computer Graphics Incorporated,
Rolling Meadows, Illinois

1991 to 1993:   Personnel Assistant
School District 25
Arlington Heights, Illinois

Education:

Bachelor's Degree in Industrial Relations

University of Illinois at Chicago Circle, June 1992

References available on request.

Margaret Chan
513 West Oakton
Mount Prospect, Illinois 60056
(847) 555-2033

Overview:

Word processing specialist, supervisor, and staff trainer seeks position in a high-growth corporate environment. Three years experience in the word processing department of a software publishing company.

Skills:

Advanced-level word processing skills with PageMaker software on the Macintosh computer and WordPerfect on IBM and IBM compatible computers

Electronic publishing and data transmission using Ventura Publisher and PageMaker

Sorting, mail merging, custom mailing, labeling, and editing of materials

Experience with inkjet and laser printers, black-and-white and color scanners, and modems

Integration of spreadsheet and database programs into word processing text and graphics programs

Employment:

1994 to Present:	Word Processing Specialist
	Farminton Publishing, Des Plaines, Illinois
1991 to 1993:	Instructor
	Oakton College, Des Plaines, Illinois

1990 to 1991:   Word Processor
                  Addison-Wesley Company, Streamwood,
                  Illinois

Education:

Associate Degree in Business/Technology

DeVry Institute of Technology, June 1990

References available upon request.

DIRECTORIES

The following directories may assist you in your job search.

BUSINESS DIRECTORIES

American Manufacturers Directory
American Manufacturers Directories
Omaha, Nebraska

CorpTech Directory of Technology Companies
Corporation Technology Information Services Incorporated
Woburn, Massachusetts

Directory of Corporate Affiliations
National Register Publishing Company
Skokie, Illinois

Dun's Directory of Service Companies
Dun's Marketing Services
Parsippany, New Jersey

International Directory of Company Histories
St. James Press
Chicago, Illinois

Service Industries, USA
Gale Research
Detroit, Michigan

Sorkins' Directory of Business and Government
Sorkin's Directories Incorporated
Chesterfield, Missouri

Thomas Register of American Manufacturers
Thomas Publishing
New York, New York

Ward's Business Directory of U.S. Private and Public Companies
Gale Research
Detroit, Michigan

SCHOOL DIRECTORIES

The Canadian Almanack and Directory
Copp Clark Publishing Company
Toronto, Ontario Canada

Directory of Canadian Universities
Association of Colleges and Universities of Canada
Altona, Ontario Canada

Directory of Public Elementary and Secondary Education Agencies
U.S. National Center for Education Statistics
Washington, D.C.

Directory of Public School Systems in the United States
Association for School, College and University Staffing
Evanston, Illinois

Handbook of Private Accredited Career Colleges and Schools
Career College Association
Washington, D.C.

Patterson's American Education
Educational Directories Incorporated
Mount Prospect, Illinois

Patterson's Private Secondary Schools
Patterson's Incorporated
Princeton, New Jersey

Private Independent Schools
Bunty and Lyon Incorporated
Wallingford, Connecticut

Private Schools in the United States
   Counsel for American Private School Education
   Washington, D.C.

INTERNSHIPS

Directory of Internships, Work Experiences, and on-the-Job Training
   Opportunities
   Ready Reference Press
   Santa Monica, California

The Princeton Review Student Access Guide to America's Top 100
   Internships
   Princeton Review
   Princeton, New Jersey